HUT

Di
Abbreviations

Other titles in the Hutchinson Pocket series:

Pocket Chronology of World Events
Pocket Dictionary of Biology
Pocket Dictionary of British History
Pocket Dictionary of Chemistry
Pocket Dictionary of Classical Music
Pocket Dictionary of Computing
Pocket Dictionary of Confusible Words
Pocket Dictionary of the Environment
Pocket Dictionary of First Names
Pocket Dictionary of Geography
Pocket Dictionary of Mathematics
Pocket Dictionary of Medical Terms
Pocket Dictionary of Physics
Pocket Dictionary of Quotations
Pocket Dictionary of Science
Pocket Dictionary of Spelling
Pocket Dictionary of 20th Century World History
Pocket Guide to Countries of the World
Pocket On This Day
Pocket Quiz Book

HUTCHINSON POCKET

Dictionary of Abbreviations

Helicon

Helicon Publishing Ltd
42 Hythe Bridge Street
Oxford OX1 2EP

Printed and bound in Great Britain by
Unwin Brothers Ltd, Old Woking, Surrey

ISBN-1-85986-007-9

British Cataloging in Publication Data

A catalogue record for this book is available
from the British Library

A

A	**ace**; used on playing cards
A	symbol for **ampere**, a unit of electric current
A	**arterial road**; used with road numbers, e.g. the A38
A	**Austria**, international vehicle registration
AA	**Alcoholics Anonymous**, a voluntary self-help organization established to combat alcoholism
AA	**antiaircraft**
AA	**Automobile Association**, a British motoring organization
AAA	**Amateur Athletic Association**, the British governing body for men's athletics
AAA	**American Automobile Association**
AAA	**antiaircraft artillery**
AAM	**air-to-air missile**
A & E	**accident and emergency**, a hospital department
A & R	**artists and repertory**, the division of a record company responsible for discovering new artists
AB	postcode for **Aberdeen**
AB	***Artium Baccalaureus*** (Latin), Bachelor of Arts, a US degree
ABA	**Amateur Boxing Association**
ABA	**American Bar Association**
ABC	**American Broadcasting Company**
ABC	**Australian Broadcasting Commission**
ABM	**anti-ballistic missile**
A-bomb	**atom bomb**
ABS	***Antiblockiersystem*** (German), an antilocking system for brakes
ABTA	**Association of British Travel Agents**
a.c.	***ante cibum*** (Latin), before meals; used in prescriptions
a/c	**account**
Ac	chemical symbol for **actinium**
AC	*(Physics)* **alternating current**
AC	***appellation contrôlée*** (French), controlled place (of origin); used on wine labels

ACAS	**Advisory, Conciliation, and Arbitration Service**, the independent body set up to improve industrial relations in Britain
acc.	*(Grammar)* **accusative**
AC/DC	*(Physics)* **alternating current/direct current**
ACLU	**American Civil Liberties Union**
ACORN	*(Computing)* **automatic checkout and recording network**
ACTH	**adrenocorticotropic hormone**, a hormone, secreted by the anterior lobe of the pituitary gland, which controls the production of corticosteroid hormones by the adrenal gland. It is commonly produced as a response to stress.
ACV	**air-cushion vehicle**
AD	***anno Domini*** (Latin), in the year of the Lord; used in dates
ADA	**Americans for Democratic Action**, an organization set up to examine legal cases involving the US Bill of Rights
A-day	**assault day**
ADC	*(Electronics)* **analogue-to-digital converter**
ADH	**antidiuretic hormone**, part of the system maintaining a correct salt/water balance in vertebrates
adj.	**adjacent**
adj.	**adjective**
adjt *or* **Adjt**	**adjutant**
Adjt-Gen	**Adjutant-General**
ADL	*(Computing)* **Ada design language**
ad lib.	***ad libitum*** (Latin), freely
Adm.	**Admiral**
ADN	**Yemen**, international vehicle registration
ADP	*(Biochemistry)* **adenosine diphosphate**, a raw material in the manufacture of adenosine triphosphate
adv.	**adverb**
advt	**advertisement**
AEA	*(UK)* **Atomic Energy Authority**
AEC	*(US)* **Atomic Energy Commission**
AEEU	**Amalgamated Engineering and Electrical Union**, a British trade union
AEF	**American Expeditionary Forces**
AEW	**airborne early warning**, a military surveillance system
AF	*(US)* **Air Force**
AFB	*(US)* **Air Force Base**

AFC **American Football Conference**
AFD **accelerated freeze-drying**, a common method of freeze-drying
AFG **Afghanistan**, international vehicle registration
AFL-CIO **American Federation of Labor and Congress of Industrial Organizations**, a federation of North American trade unions
AFM *(Physics)* **atomic force microscope**
afp *or* **AFP** **alphafetoprotein**, a protein found in amniotic fluid, which can indicate a foetal abnormality such as spina bifida
AFT **American Federation of Teachers**
AFV **armoured fighting vehicle**
Ag chemical symbol for **silver**
AG *Aktiengesellschaft* (German), public limited company
AG **Attorney-General**
AGM **air-to-ground missile**
AGM **annual general meeting**
AGR **advanced gas-cooled reactor**, a type of nuclear reactor
AI **artificial insemination**
AI **artificial intelligence**, the branch of science concerned with creating computer programs that can perform actions comparable with those of an intelligent human
AID **Agency for International Development**
AID **artificial insemination by donor**
Aids *or* **AIDS** **acquired immune deficiency syndrome**, a sexually transmitted disease caused by the human immunodeficiency virus (HIV)
AIH **artificial insemination by husband**
air con **air conditioning**; used in car advertisements
AK postcode for **Alaska**, a US state
AK **automatic Kalashnikov**, a rifle
a.k.a. *or* **AKA** **also known as**
Al chemical symbol for **aluminium**
AL postcode for **Alabama**, a US state
AL **Albania**, international vehicle registration
AL *(Baseball)* **American League**
AL postcode for **St Albans**
Ala. **Alabama**, a US state

ALA **all letters answered**; used in newspaper lonely hearts advertisements

ALA **American Library Association**

ALADI **Asociación Latino-Americana de Integración** (Spanish), Latin American Integration Association, an organization aiming to create a common market in Latin America

Alas. **Alaska**, a US state

ALAWP **all letters answered with photograph**; used in newspaper lonely hearts advertisements

ALBM **air-launched ballistic missile**

ALCM **air-launched cruise missile**

A level *(Education)* **Advanced level**, an examination taken at the age of 18 in the UK

ALF **Animal Liberation Front**

ALGOL *(Computing)* **algorithmic language**, an early high-level programming language

ALP **Australian Labor Party**, a moderate left-of-centre political party

alt. **altitude**

ALU *(Computing)* **arithmetic and logic unit**, the part of the central processing unit that performs the basic arithmetic and logic operations on data

a.m. ***ante meridiem*** (Latin), before noon

Am chemical symbol for **americium**

AM **amplitude modulation**, a method by which radio waves are altered for the transmission of broadcasting signals

AM ***Artium Magister*** (Latin), Master of Arts, a US degree

A.M. ***ante meridiem*** (Latin), before noon

AMA **American Medical Association**

Amex (trademark) **American Express**

AMF **Allied Mobile Force**, a permanent multinational military force, ready to move immediately to any NATO country

amp. **ampere**, a unit of electrical current

Amraam **advanced medium-range air-to-air missile**

AMVETS **American Veterans of World War II and Korea**

ANA **All Nippon Airways**, a Japanese airline

ANC **African National Congress**, a South African nationalist organization

AND **Andorra**, international vehicle registration

ANSI **American National Standards Institute**, the US body

	that sets official procedures, in computing and electronics for example
a/nw	**as new**; used in car advertisements
Anzac	**Australian and New Zealand Army Corps**, in World War I
ANZUS	**Australia, New Zealand, and the United States**, a military alliance replaced in 1954 by the South East Asia Treaty Organization (SEATO)
a.o.b. *or* **AOB**	**any other business**; used at the end of the agenda for a meeting
AOC	***appellation d'origine contrôlée*** (French) controlled place of origin; used on wine labels
AONB	**area of outstanding natural beauty**
AOR	**adult-oriented rock**
a.p.	***ante prandium*** (Latin), before a meal; used in prescriptions
a.p.	**atmospheric pressure**
AP	**armour-piercing**
AP	**Associated Press**, the world's largest news service
APA	**American Psychiatric Association**
APB	**all points bulletin**, a police alert
APC	**armoured personnel carrier**, a military vehicle designed to transport up to ten people
APC	**aspirin, phenacetin, and caffeine**, constituents of a painkilling pill
APEX	**Advance-Purchase Excursion**, a reduced fare on a train or aeroplane
API	*(Computing)* **application programmer interface**
APL	*(Computing)* **A Programming Language**
APO	*(US)* **army post office**
approx.	**approximately**
APR	**annual percentage rate**, a charge for granting consumer credit
apt.	**apartment**
APT	**advanced passenger train**
AQMG	**Assistant Quartermaster General**
Ar	chemical symbol for **argon**
AR	postcode for **Arkansas**, a US state
ARC	**Aids-related complex**

ARC **American Red Cross**
Ariz. **Arizona**, a US state
Ark. **Arkansas**, a US state
ARM **antiradiation (anti-radar) missile**
ARMS **Action for Research into Multiple Sclerosis**
ARP **air-raid precautions**
Arpanet *or* **ARPANET** *(Computing)* **Advanced Research Projects Agency Network**
arr. **arranged** (by); used in music
arr. **arrival** *or* **arrive(s)**
ARV **American Revised Version of the Bible**
As chemical symbol for **arsenic**
AS **antisubmarine**
ASA **Advertising Standards Authority**, a British organization that promotes higher standards of advertising in the media, excluding television and radio
ASA *(Photography)* a numbering system for rating the speed of films, devised by the American Standards Association, superseded by ISO
a.s.a.p. **as soon as possible**
ASAT **antisatellite weapon**
ASBAH **Association for Spina Bifida and Hydrocephalus**
ASBM **air-to-surface ballistic missile**
ASCAP **American Society of Composers, Authors, and Publishers**, a US performing rights society
ASCII *(Computing)* **American Standard Code for Information Interchange**, a coding system in which numbers are assigned to letters, digits, and punctuation symbols
ASE **American Stock Exchange**
ASEAN **Association of South East Asian Nations**, established in 1967. The members are Indonesia, Malaysia, the Philippines, Singapore, Thailand, and Brunei.
ASH **Action on Smoking and Health**
ASL **American Sign Language**
Aslef *or* **ASLEF** **Associated Society of Locomotive Engineers and Firemen**, a British trade union
AS level *(Education)* **Advanced Supplementary level**, an intermediate examination taken by British 18-year-olds

ASM	**air-to-surface missile**
ASPAC	**Asian and Pacific Council**, established in 1966 to encourage cultural and economic cooperation in Oceania and Asia
ASPCA	**American Society for Prevention of Cruelty to Animals**
assoc.	**associated** *or* **association**
ASSR	**Autonomous Soviet Socialist Republic**
AST	**Atlantic Standard Time**
ASV	**American Standard Version of the Bible**
At	chemical symbol for **astatine**
AT	**achievement test**
AT	**Atlantic Time**
AT	*(Education)* **attainment target**
ATAF	**Allied Tactical Air Force**
AT & T	**American Telephone and Telegraph**, a US telecommunications company
ATB	**advanced technology bomber**
ATBM	**antitactical ballistic missile**
ATC	**Air Training Corps**
ATL	**Association of Teachers and Lecturers**
ATM	**automated teller machine**
at. no.	**atomic number**
ATO	**assisted takeoff**
ATOL	**Air Travel Organizers' Licence**
ATP	**adenosine triphosphate**, a nucleotide molecule found in all cells
Att-Gen	**Attorney-General**
ATV	**all-terrain vehicle**
Au	chemical symbol for **gold**
AUM	**air-to-underwater missile**
AUS	**Army of the United States**
AUS	**Australia**, international vehicle registration
AUT	**Association of University Teachers**, a British trade union
av.	**average**
Av.	**avenue**
AV	**audiovisual**
AV	**Authorized Version of the Bible**
Ave.	**avenue**
AVM	**Air Vice-Marshal**

AVR **Army Volunteer Reserve**
AWACS **Airborne Warning and Control System**, a surveillance system that incorporates a long-range radar mounted on an aircraft
AWL **absent with leave**
AWOL **absent without (official) leave**
AZ postcode for **Arizona**, a US state
AZT **azidothymidine**, an antiviral drug used in the treatment of AIDS

B

b.	*(Cricket)* **bowled by**
b.	*(Cricket)* **bye**
B	**Belgium**, international vehicle registration
B	postcode for **Birmingham**
B	*(Chess)* **bishop**
B	**black**; used on pencils
B	chemical symbol for **boron**
B	symbol for secondary road; used with road numbers, e.g. the B4020
Ba	chemical symbol for **barium**
BA	**Bachelor of Arts**
BA	postcode for **Bath**
BA	**British Academy**
BA	**British Airways**
BAA	**British Airports Authority**
BAAF	**British Agencies for Adoption and Fostering**
BAAS	**British Association for the Advancement of Science**
BAe	**British Aerospace**
BAFTA	**British Academy of Film and Television Arts**
BAGA	**British Amateur Gymnastics Association**
BALPA	**British Airline Pilots' Association**
b. and b. *or* **B & B**	**bed and breakfast**
B & W	**black and white**
BAOR	**British Army of the Rhine**
Bapt.	**Baptist**
BARB	**Broadcasters' Audience Research Board**
Bart.	**Baronet**
Bart's	**St Bartholomew's Hospital**, in London
BASIC	*(Computing)* **Beginner's All-purpose Symbolic Instruction Code**, a programming language
BASW	**British Association of Social Workers**
bb.	*(Baseball)* **base on balls**

BB	postcode for **Blackburn**
BBBC	**British Boxing Board of Control**
BBC	**British Broadcasting Corporation**, the British state-owned broadcasting network
BBFC	**British Board of Film Censors**
BBQ	**barbecue**
BC	**before Christ**; used for dates in the Christian calendar
BC	**British Columbia**, a Canadian province
BCCI	**Bank of Credit and Commerce International**, an international bank
BCD	*(Computing)* **binary-coded decimal**
BCE	**before the common era**; used for dates as an alternative to BC
BCF	**British Chess Federation**
BCF	**British Cycling Federation**
BCG	**bacillus of Calmette and Guérin**, used as a vaccine to confer active immunity to tuberculosis
BCNZ	**Broadcasting Corporation of New Zealand**
BCPL	**Basic Computer Programming Language**
BD	**Bangladesh**, international vehicle registration
BD	postcode for **Bradford**
BDA	**British Deaf Association**
BDA	**British Dental Association**
BDA	**British Diabetic Association**
bdrm	**bedroom**
BDS	**Barbados**, international vehicle registration
Be	chemical symbol for **beryllium**
BE	*(US)* **Board of Education**
BEA	**British Epilepsy Association**
BEAB	**British Electrical Approvals Board**
BEd	**Bachelor of Education**
Beds	**Bedfordshire**, an English county
BEM	**British Empire Medal**
Benelux	**Belgium, the Netherlands, Luxembourg**, a customs union that was the precursor of the European Community
Berks	**Berkshire**, an English county
BFI	**British Film Institute**, an organization created to promote the cinema as a means of entertainment and instruction
BFPO	**British Forces Post Office**

BG	**Brigadier General**
BG	**Bulgaria**, international vehicle registration
BH	**Belize**, international vehicle registration
BH	postcode for **Bournemouth**
BHF	**British Heart Foundation**
bhp	**brake horsepower**
BHS	**British Home Stores**, a department store
Bi	chemical symbol for **bismuth**
b.i.d.	***bis in die*** (Latin), twice a day; used in prescriptions
BIM	**British Institute of Management**
BIOS	*(Computing)* **basic input-output system**
BIS	**Bank for International Settlements**, a forum for European central banks
bit	*(Computing)* **binary digit**, the smallest unit of data stored in a computer
Bk	chemical symbol for **berkelium**
BL	postcode for **Bolton**
bldg	**building**
BLT	**bacon, lettuce, and tomato, a sandwich filling**
Blvd	**boulevard**
BM	**British Museum**, Britain's largest museum
BMA	**British Medical Association**
BMC	**British Medical Council**
BMDO	**Ballistic Missile Defence Organization**, the name of the Strategic Defense Initiative since May 1993
BMEWS	**ballistic missile early warning system**
BMI	**Broadcast Music Incorporated**, a US performing rights society
BMJ	**British Medical Journal**
BMR	**basal metabolic rate**, the amount of energy needed just to stay alive
BMW	**Bayerische Motorenwerke**, a German car manufacturer
BMX	**bicycle motocross**
Bn	**Baron**
BN	postcode for **Brighton**
BNF	**British Nuclear Fuels**
BNOC	**British National Oil Corporation**
BNOC	**British National Opera Company**
BNP	***Banque nationale de Paris***, the National Bank of Paris
BO	**body odour**

BOA **British Olympic Association**
BOC **British Oxygen Corporation**
BOF *(Computing)* **beginning of file**
B of E **Bank of England**
bor. **borough**
BOSS *(South Africa)* **Bureau of State Security**
BoT *or* **BOT** **Board of Trade**, part of the British Department of Trade and Industry
BOT marker *(Computing)* **beginning of tape marker**
BP **blood pressure**
BP **boiling point**
BP **British Petroleum**
BP **British Pharmacopoeia**
BPAS **British Pregnancy Advisory Service**
bpi *(Computing)* **bits per inch**
BPIF **British Printing Industries' Federation**
BPOE *(US)* **Benevolent and Protective Order of Elks**
bps *(Computing)* **bits per second**
Bq symbol for **becquerel**, a unit of radioactivity
Br chemical symbol for **bromine**
BR **Brazil**, international vehicle registration
BR **British Rail**
BR postcode for **Bromley**
BRA **British Rheumatism and Arthritis Association**
BRCS **British Red Cross Society**
BRN **Bahrain**, international vehicle registration
BRS **British Road Services**
BRU **Brunei**, international vehicle registration
BS **Bachelor of Science**, a US degree
BS **Bahamas**, international vehicle registration
BS postcode for **Bristol**
BS **British Standard**, catalogue or publication number
BS **building society**
BSA **Boy Scouts of America**
BSc **Bachelor of Science**
BSC **British Steel Corporation**
BSC **British Sugar Corporation**
BSC **Broadcasting Standards Council**, the British body concerned with handling complaints on treatment of sex and violence in television and radio programmes

BSE **bovine spongiform encephalopathy**, a disease of cattle that renders the brain spongy and may drive an animal mad. It is commonly known as mad cow disease.

BSI **British Standards Institution**, the British national standards body, which tests and sets standards for consumer goods

BSkyB **British Sky Broadcasting**, a group of satellite TV channels

BSM **British School of Motoring**

BST **bovine somatotropin**, a hormone that is injected into cows to increase their milk yield, but which has not been proved to be harmless to humans

BST **British Summer Time**

Bt **Baronet**

BT postcode for **Belfast**

BT **British Telecom**, a company that is responsible for telecommunications, including the telephone network, and the viewdata network, Prestel

BTA **British Tourist Authority**

BTG **British Technology Group**, a corporation exploiting inventions derived from public or private sources

bth **bath** *or* **bathroom**

BThU *or* **Btu** **British thermal unit**, an imperial unit of heat, replaced by the joule

BUAV **British Union for the Abolition of Vivisection**

Bucks **Buckinghamshire**, an English county

BUPA **British United Provident Association**, a health insurance company

BUR **Burma**, international vehicle registration

BVA **British Veterinary Association**

b/w **black and white**

BW **biological warfare**

BW **British Waterways**

B/W **black and white**

BWR **boiling-water reactor**

C

c. *(Cricket)* **caught**

c. ***circa*** (Latin), about; used with dates that are uncertain, e.g. Born c.1603

C *(Computing)* a general-purpose programming language that was developed in the 1970s and is closely associated with the Unix operating system

C chemical symbol for **carbon**

C **Conservative**, a member or supporter of the British Conservative party

C symbol for **coulomb**, a unit of electric charge

C **Cuba**, international vehicle registration

C Roman numeral for **100**

°C symbol for **degrees Celsius**, commonly called centigrade

C4 **Channel 4**, a British television channel

Ca chemical symbol for **calcium**

CA postcode for **California**, a US state

CA postcode for **Carlisle**

CA **Central America**

CAA **Civil Aviation Authority**

CAB **Citizens' Advice Bureau**, a British organization that provides information and advice to the public on any subject, such as personal or financial problems

CAB *(US)* **Civil Aeronautics Board**

CACM **Central American Common Market**, an economic alliance established in 1960. Members are El Salvador, Guatemala, Nicaragua and Costa Rica.

CAD **computer-aided design**, used in architecture, electronics, and engineering to test designs or give three-dimensional views of them

cal symbol for **calorie**, a unit of heat, replaced by the joule

Cal. **California**, a US state

CAL **computer-assisted learning**, the use of computers in education and training

Calif.	**California**, a US state
Caltech	**California Institute of Technology**
CAM	**computer-aided manufacture**
Cambs	**Cambridgeshire**, an English county
CAMRA	**Campaign for Real Ale**
c & b	*(Cricket)* **caught and bowled**
C & E	**Customs and Excise**
C & G	**City and Guilds**
C. and W.	*(Music)* **country and western**
Cantab	***Cantabrigiensis*** (Latin), of Cambridge; used after degrees from Cambridge University
cap.	*(Printing)* **capital letter**
CAP	*(US)* **Civil Air Patrol**
CAP	**Common Agricultural Policy**, a system that allows European Community countries to organize and control their agricultural production jointly
Caps	**capitals**; used on a keyboard
CARD	**Campaign Against Racial Discrimination**
CARE	**Christian Action for Research and Education**
CARE	**Cooperative for American Relief Everywhere**
CARICOM	**Caribbean Community and Common Market**, established in 1973 to coordinate economic and foreign policy in the Caribbean region
CAT	**Centre for Alternative Technology**
CAT	**computerized axial tomography**, a medical technique for looking inside bodies without disturbing them, by taking cross-sectional slices from X-ray scans
CATV	**community antenna television**
c/b	*(Cricket)* **caught and bowled**
CB	postcode for **Cambridge**
CB	**citizens' band**; used for short-range radio communication
CB	**Companion of the Order of the Bath**
CBC	**Canadian Broadcasting Corporation**, the national radio and television service of Canada
CBE	**Commander of the Order of the British Empire**
CBI	**Confederation of British Industry**, an organization of employers
CBS	**Columbia Broadcasting System**, a US television and radio network
CBW	**chemical and biological warfare**

cc symbol for **cubic centimetre**, a unit of volume
CC **cricket club**
CC **County Council**
CCF **Combined Cadet Force**
CCHE **Central Council for Health Education**
CCTV **closed-circuit television**
CCU **coronary care unit**
ccw. **counterclockwise**
cd symbol for **candela**, a unit of luminous intensity
Cd chemical symbol for **cadmium**
CD **Centrum Democraten**, Centre Democrats, a Dutch extreme right political party
CD **Centrum-Demokraterne**, Centre Democrats, a Danish moderate centrist political party
CD *(US)* **Civil Defense**
CD **compact disc**
CD **Corps Diplomatique** (French), Diplomatic Corps
CDA **Christen-Democratisch Appel**, Christian Democratic Appeal, a Dutch right-of-centre political party
CD-I *(Computing)* **compact disc-interactive**, which provides multimedia programs for the home user
CDN **Canada**, international vehicle registration
CD-ROM *(Computing)* **compact-disc read-only memory**, a way of storing information such as written text or pictures, ideal for large works such as encyclopedias
CDS **Centro Democrático E Social**, Democratic and Social Centre, a Spanish centrist political party
CDS **Partido do Centro Democrático**, Party of the Democratic Centre, a Portuguese moderate left-of-centre political party
CDT *(US)* **Central Daylight Time**
CDT **Craft, Design, and Technology**
CDU **Christlich Demokratische Union**, Christian Democratic Union, a German centre-right party
Ce chemical symbol for **cerium**
CE **Church of England**
CE **Common Era**; used for dates as an alternative to AD
CEGB **Central Electricity Generating Board**
CentCom **Central Command**, a US military strike force
CEO **Chief Executive Officer**

CERN **Conseil européen pour la recherche nucléaire** (French), a nuclear research organization founded as a cooperative enterprise among European governments
cert. **certificate**
cert. **certification**
cert. **certified**
CET **Central European Time**
cf. *(Baseball)* **centre fielder**
cf. ***confer*** (Latin), compare; used in written texts
c.f. **cost and freight**
Cf chemical symbol for **californium**
CF postcode for **Cardiff**
CF **cost and freight**
CF **cystic fibrosis**
CFC **chlorofluorocarbon**, a chemical used in aerosols and refrigerators, which is partly responsible for the destruction of the ozone layer
CFE **College of Further Education**
CFE **Conventional Forces in Europe**, talks which began in 1989 to reduce non-nuclear forces in Europe
c.f.i. *or*
CFI **cost, freight, and insurance**
ch. *(Chess)* **check**
c/h **central heating**
Ch. **Church**
CH postcode for **Chester**
CH **Companion of Honour**, a British order of chivalry
CH **Switzerland**, international vehicle registration
C/H **central heating**
chap. **chapter**
CHAR **Campaign for Homeless People** (formerly Campaign for the Homeless and Rootless)
CHDL **computer hardware description language**
CHE **Campaign for Homosexual Equality**
Ches **Cheshire**, an English county
Chr. *or*
Chron. *(Bible)* **Chronicles**
CHSA **Chest, Heart, and Stroke Association**
CI **Channel Islands**
CI **Ivory Coast**, international vehicle registration

CIA **Central Intelligence Agency**, a US government organization established in 1947 to operate or gather intelligence overseas

CID **Criminal Investigation Department**, the detective branch of British police forces

cif **cost, insurance, and freight** *or* **charged in full**; many countries value their imports on this basis

CIFE **Colleges and Institutes of Further Education**

CIO *(US)* **Congress of Industrial Organizations**

CIP *(US)* **Cataloging in Publication**

CIPFA **Chartered Institute of Public Finance and Accountancy**

CIS **Commonwealth of Independent States**, the successor body to the USSR, established in 1992 by Armenia, Azerbaijan, Belarus, Kazakhstan, Kyrgyzstan, Moldova, the Russian Federation, Tajikistan, Turkmenistan, Ukraine, and Uzbekistan

CISC **complex instruction set computer**, a microprocessor that offers a large number of instructions

CITES **Convention on International Trade in Endangered Species**, an international agreement that prohibits the trade in endangered species

CIU **Club and Institute Union**

CIWF **Compassion in World Farming**

CJD **Creutzfeldt-Jakob Disease**, a disease in humans in which the brain becomes spongy, leading to dementia

ckw. **clockwise**

cl **centilitre**

Cl chemical symbol for **chlorine**

CL **Sri Lanka**, international vehicle registration

Clev **Cleveland**, an English county

Cllr **Councillor**

c/lock **central locking**; used in car advertisements

CLP **Constituency Labour Party**

CLU **Chartered Life Underwriter**

CLU *(US)* **Civil Liberties Union**

cm **centimetre**

Cm chemical symbol for **curium**

CM postcode for **Chelmsford**

CMV *(Medicine)* **cytomegalovirus**

CMYK **cyan magenta yellow key**; used to describe colour printers
CNAA **Council for National Academic Awards**
CND **Campaign for Nuclear Disarmament**, a British organization launched in 1958
CNN **Cable News Network**, an international television news channel
CNN **Certified Nursery Nurse**
CNO **Chief of Naval Operations**
CNS **central nervous system**
co. **company**
c/o **care of**; used in addressing letters
Co chemical symbol for **cobalt**
Co. **Colorado**, a US state
CO postcode for **Colchester**
CO **Colombia**, international vehicle registration
CO postcode for **Colorado**, a US state
CO **Commanding Officer**
Cobol *or* **COBOL** **common business-oriented language**, a high-level computer-programming language designed in the late 1950s for business use
COC **combined oral contraceptive**
c.o.d. *or* **COD** **cash on delivery**
COD **chemical oxygen demand**, a measure of water and effluent quality
C of C **Chamber of Commerce**
C of E **Church of England**
Cohse *or* **COHSE** **Confederation of Health Service Employees**, a British trade union
COI **Central Office of Information**, a British government department responsible for the operation of government information services
COIN **counter insurgency**, the suppression by a state's armed forces of uprisings against the state
Col. **Colorado**, a US state
Col. *(Bible)* **Colossians**
COL **computer-oriented language**
COL **cost of living**

COLA *(US)* **cost-of-living adjustment**; used in a union contract to give workers an automatic pay rise to match inflation
Colo. **Colorado**, a US state
Coloss. *(Bible)* **Colossians**
cols **columns**
COMA **Committee on Medical Aspects of Food Policy**
COMAL *(Computing)* **common algorithmic language**
Comecon **Council for Mutual Economic Assistance**, which existed 1949–91. Members included the USSR, Bulgaria, Czechoslovakia, Hungary, Poland, Romania, East Germany, Mongolia, Cuba, and Vietnam.
COMEX **Commodity Exchange**, in New York
Cominform **Communist Information Bureau**, which existed 1947–56, to exchange information between European Communist parties
COMINT **communications intelligence**
Comintern **Communist International**, formed by Lenin in Moscow, which advocated a popular front against Hitler from 1933
Comsat *or* **COMSAT** **communications satellite**
Com. Ver. **Common Version**, of the Bible
Con. **Conservative**, a member or supporter of the British Conservative party
Confed. *(US)* **Confederate**
conj. *(Grammar)* **conjugation**
conj. **conjunction**
conj. **conjunctive**
Conn. **Connecticut**, a US state
Conrail *or* **ConRail** *(US)* **Consolidated Rail Corporation**
cont. **continued**
co-op **cooperative**
Cor. *(Bible)* **Corinthians**
CORE **Congress of Racial Equality**, a US nonviolent civil rights organization
Corn **Cornwall**, an English county
cos *(Maths)* **cosine**
c.o.s. *or* **COS** **cash on shipment**
COS **Chief of Staff**

cosec *(Maths)* **cosecant**
cosech *(Maths)* **hyperbolic cosecant**
cosh *(Maths)* **hyperbolic cosine**
cot *or* **cotan** *(Maths)* **cotangent**
CP **Communist Party**
CPAC **Consumer Protection Advisory Committee**
CPAG **Child Poverty Action Group**
c.p.h. **cycles per hour**
CPI **consumer price index**
CPR *(Medicine)* **cardiopulmonary resuscitation**
CPRE **Council for the Protection of Rural England**, a countryside conservation group
CPS **Crown Prosecution Service**
CPSA **Civil and Public Services Association**, a British clerical civil servants' union
CPSA **Conservative Party of South Africa**, an extreme right political party
CPU **central processing unit**, the main component of a computer
CPVE **Certificate of Pre-Vocational Education**, an educational qualification introduced in Britain in 1986 for students over 16
Cr chemical symbol for **chromium**
CR **Costa Rica**, international vehicle registration
CR postcode for **Croydon**
CRC *(US)* **Civil Rights Commission**
CRAC **Careers Research and Advisory Centre**
CRC **camera-ready copy**
CRC **Cancer Research Campaign**
CRC **Community Relations Council**
CRE **Commission for Racial Equality**
CRMF **Cancer Relief Macmillan Fund**
CRO **Criminal Records Office**
CRT **cathode-ray tube**, a vacuum tube in which a beam of electrons is produced and focused onto a fluorescent screen
CRW **counter-revolutionary warfare**
CS **Chief of Staff**
CS **Christian Science** *or* **Christian Scientist**
CS **(US) Civil Service**

CSA	**Child Support Agency**, a UK government agency that carries out the assessment, review, collection, and enforcement of maintenance payments from absent parents
CSA	**Confederate States of America**
CSCE	**Conference on Security and Cooperation in Europe**, also known as the Helsinki Conference
CSE	**Certificate of Secondary Education**, an examination taken by British secondary school pupils who were not regarded as academically capable of GCE O level. Replaced by the GCSE in 1988.
CSEU	**Confederation of Shipbuilding and Engineering Unions**
CST	**Central Standard Time**
CSU	**Christlich Soziale Union**, Christian Social Union, a German right-of-centre political party
CSU	**Civil Service Union**
CSV	**community service volunteer**
CSYS	*(Scotland)* **Certificate of Sixth Year Studies**
Ct.	**Connecticut**, a US state
CT	postcode for **Canterbury**
CT	**Central Time**
CT	**computerized tomography**
CT	postcode for **Connecticut**, a US state
CTC	**city technology college**, a British school funded jointly by government and industry, designed to teach technological subjects to 11- to 18-year-olds in inner-city areas
CTOL	**conventional takeoff and landing**
Ctrl	**control**; used on a keyboard
CTV	**Canadian Television Network Limited**
cu	**cubic**
Cu	chemical symbol for **copper**
Cumb	**Cumbria**, an English county
CUP	**Cambridge University Press**
c.v.	***cheval-vapeur*** (French), horsepower; used for car models, e.g. Citroën 2CV
c.v.	**curriculum vitae**
CV	***cheval-vapeur*** (French), horsepower; used for car models, e.g. Citroën 2CV
CV	**Common Version**, of the Bible
CV	postcode for **Coventry**
CV	**curriculum vitae**

CVP	**Christelijke Volkspartij** (Flemish), Christian Social Party, a Belgian centre-left political party, also known as Parti Social Chrétien (French)
CVS	**chorionic villus sampling**, where a sample of tissue from the placenta is taken to test for genetic abnormalities of the fetus
cw.	**clockwise**
CW	**chemical warfare**
CW	postcode for **Crewe**
CWA	**Crime Writers Association**
c.w.o.	**cash with order**
CWO	**chief warrant officer**
cwt	symbol for **hundredweight**, a unit of weight
CY	**Cyprus**, international vehicle registration
CYO	**Catholic Youth Organization**
CZ	**Canal Zone**

D

d. — **day**
d. — **diameter**
d. — **died**
d. — ***denarius*** (Latin), penny or pennies; used in Britain before decimalization
D — **Democrat**, a member or supporter of the US Democratic Party
D — **Duchess**
D — **Duke**
D — **Germany**; international vehicle registration
D — Roman numeral for **500**
DA — postcode for **Dartford**
DA — **Department of Agriculture**, a US government department
DA — *(US)* **District Attorney**
DAC — *(Computing)* **digital-to-analogue converter**
DAGMAR — **defined advertising goals for measured advertising results**
Dan. — *(Bible)* **Daniel**
D and C — **dilatation and curettage**, a common gynaecological procedure in which the cervix (neck of the womb) is widened, giving access so that the lining of the womb can be scraped away, for instance after a miscarriage or for biopsy
d and d — **drunk and disorderly**
DAP — *(Computing)* **distributed array processor**
DAR — **Daughters of the American Revolution**, a society of women descended from patriots of the Revolutionary War
dat. — *(Grammar)* **dative**
DAT — *(Medicine)* **dementia of the Alzheimer type**
DAT — **digital audio tape**
dB — symbol for **decibel**, a unit of sound intensity
DB — **Deutsche Bundesbank**, the German Federal Bank

DBE	**Dame Commander of the Order of the British Empire**
DBib	**Douay Bible**
dbl. *or* **dble**	**double**
DBS	**direct broadcast satellite**
DC	**Detective Constable**
DC	*(Physics)* **direct current**
DC	**District Commissioner**
DC	**District of Columbia**, federal district of the USA
DC	**Douglas Commercial**; used on aircraft, e.g. the DC8
DCB	**Dame Commander of the Order of the Bath**
DCC	*(Computing)* **digital compact cassette**
DCI	**Detective Chief Inspector**
DCM	*(US)* **Distinguished Conduct Medal**
DD	**Doctor of Divinity**
DD	postcode for **Dundee**
DDC	*(Computing)* **direct digital control**
DDL	*(Computing)* **data description language**
DDR	**Deutsche Demokratische Republik**, German Democratic Republic, the former East Germany
DDT	**dichlorodiphenyl-trichloroethane**, an insecticide that is highly toxic
DE	postcode for **Delaware**, a US state
DE	**Department of Employment**, a British government department
DE	postcode for **Derby**
decd	**deceased**
def.	**definite**
def.	**definition**
DEFCON	*(Military)* **defence readiness condition**
deg.	**degree**
Del.	**Delaware**, a US state
Del	**delete**; used on a keyboard
Dem.	*(US)* **Democrat** *or* **Democratic**
DemU	**Democratic Unionist**, member of the Northern Ireland political party
den	**denier**, measure of thickness of tights or stockings
DEN	**District Enrolled Nurse**
dep.	**departure**
dep.	**deputy**
dept	**department**

Derby *or*
Derbys **Derbyshire**, an English county
DES *(Computing)* **data encryption standard**
DES **Department of Education and Science**, the former name for the British Department for Education
Det **Detective**
DET **diethyltryptamine**, a hallucinogenic drug
Det Con **Detective Constable**
Det Insp **Detective Inspector**
Det Sgt **Detective Sergeant**
Det Supt **Detective Superintendent**
Deut. *(Bible)* **Deuteronomy**
Devon **Devonshire**, an English county
DEW *(Military)* **distant early warning**
DFC *(US)* **Distinguished Flying Cross**
DFE **Department for Education**, a British government department
DFM *(US)* **Distinguished Flying Medal**
DG ***Deo gratias*** (Latin), thanks be to God
DG postcode for **Dumfries**
DGAA **Distressed Gentlefolks Aid Association**
DH **Department of Health**, a British government department
DH postcode for **Durham**
DHA **District Health Authority**
DHSS **Department of Health and Social Security**, a former British government department, split into two parts in 1988, the Department of Health and the Department of Social Security
di. **diameter**
DI *(US)* **Department of the Interior**
DI **Detective Inspector**
DI **donor insemination**
DI *(US)* **drill instructor**
dia. **diameter**
diag. **diagram**
diam. **diameter**
DIANE **Direct Information Access Network for Europe**, a collection of information suppliers or 'hosts', for the European computer network
dict. **dictation**

dict. **dictionary**
DIG **Deputy Inspector-General**
dil. **dilute** *or* **diluted**
DIN **Deutsches Institut für Normung**, the German national standards body, which has set standards for paper sizes and electrical connectors
Dip **Diploma**; used in qualifications
dir. **directed, direction** *or* **director**
dismac *(Military)* **digital scene-matching area correlation sensors**
div. **divorced**
diy *or* **DIY** **do-it-yourself**
d.j. **dinner jacket**
d.j. **disc jockey**
DJ **dinner jacket**
DJ **disc jockey**
DJ *(US)* **District Judge**
DJI **Dow Jones Index**, the New York Stock Exchange index
DJIA **Dow Jones Industrial Average**, an index based on the prices of 30 major companies
DK **Denmark**, international vehicle registration
dl **decilitre**
DL postcode for **Darlington**
DLO **dead letter office**
DLR **Docklands Light Railway**
dly **daily**
dm **decimetre**
DM **Deutschmark**, the German unit of currency
DMA *(Computing)* **direct memory access**
D-mark **Deutschmark**, the German unit of currency
DMD *(Medicine)* **Duchenne muscular dystrophy**
DMT **dimethyltryptamine**, a hallucinogenic drug
DMZ **demilitarized zone**
DN postcode for **Doncaster**
DNA **deoxyribonucleic acid**, a complex molecule that contains all the information needed for a living organism
DNC *(Computing)* **distributed numerical control**
DNR **do not resuscitate**
do. **ditto**
DOA **dead on arrival**

d.o.b. *or* **DOB** **date of birth**
doc. **document**
Doc. **Doctor**
DOC ***Denominazione di Origine Controllata*** (Italian), name of origin controlled; used on wine labels
DOD **Department of Defense**, a US government department
d.o.e. **depends on experience**; used in job advertisements
DoE **Department of the Environment**, a British government department
DOE **Department of Employment**, a British government department
DOE **Department of Energy**, a US government department
DOE **Department of the Environment**, a British government department
DoH *or* **DOH** **Department of Health**, a British government department
DoI *or* **DOI** **Department of Industry**, a British government department
DOI *(Computing)* **document oriented interface**
Dom. **Dominican**
DOM ***Deo Optimo Maximo*** (Latin), to God, the best, the greatest
DOM **Dominican Republic**, international vehicle registration
Dors **Dorset**, an English county
DOS *(Computing)* **disc operating system**, an operating system specifically designed for use with disc storage
DoT **Department of Transport**, a British government department
d.o.w. *or* **DOW** **died of wounds**
doz. **dozen**
d.p. ***directione propria*** (Latin), with proper direction; used in prescriptions
DP **data processing**, the use of computers for performing clerical tasks such as stock control, payroll, and dealing with orders
DP **Democratic Party**, a South African left-of-centre multiracial political party
DP **displaced person**
DPhil **Doctor of Philosophy**
dpi *(Computing)* **dots per inch**
dpl. **diplomat**

DPMI *(Computing)* **DOS Protected Mode Interface**
DPP **Director of Public Prosecutions**, the head of the Crown Prosecution Service in Britain, responsible for the conduct of all criminal prosecutions in England and Wales
DPT **diphtheria, pertussis** (whooping cough)**, tetanus**, a combined vaccine
Dr **Director**
Dr **Doctor**
Dr **Drive**; used in street names
DR **dead reckoning**; used in navigation
DR **Democratic Renewal**, a Greek political party
DR **dining room**
DRAM *(Computing)* **dynamic random-access memory**, a form of silicon chip memory
DRAW *(Computing)* **direct read after write**
DRDW *(Computing)* **direct read during write**
DS **Detective Sergeant**
DS *(Medicine)* **Down's syndrome**
DSc **Doctor of Science**
DSC *(US)* **Distinguished Service Cross**
DSM *(US)* **Distinguished Service Medal**
DSO **Distinguished Service Order**, a British military medal
DSP *(Computing)* **digital signal processor**
DSS **Department of Social Security**, a British government department
DST *(US)* **Daylight Saving Time**
DST *(UK)* **Double Summer Time**
DT postcode for **Dorchester**
d.t.b.a. **date to be advised**
DTD *(Computing)* **document type definition**
DTE *(Computing)* **data terminal equipment**
DTI **Department of Trade and Industry**, a British government department
DTp **Department of Transport**, a British government department
DTP **desktop publishing**, the use of microcomputers for small-scale typesetting and page make-up
d.t.'s *or* **DT's** *(Medicine)* **delirium tremens**, a psychotic condition characterized by tremor, anxiety, and hallucinations, occurring in some cases of chronic alcoholism

Du	**Duke**
dup.	**duplicate**
DUP	**Democratic Unionist Party**, a Northern Ireland right-of-centre political party
Dur	**Durham**, an English county
DV	*Deo volente* (Latin), God willing
DV	**Douay Version**, of the Bible
DVLA	**Driver and Vehicle Licensing Authority**
d.w.	**dead weight**
DWA	**driving without awareness** (an offence)
dwt	**pennyweight**
d.w.t. *or* **DWT**	**dead-weight tonnage**
Dy	chemical symbol for **dysprosium**
DY	**Benin**, international vehicle registration
DY	postcode for **Dudley**
dz.	**dozen**
DZ	**Algeria**, international vehicle registration

E

e.	*(Baseball)* **error**
E	**Earl**
E	**earth**; used on electrical circuits
E	**east**
E	postcode for **east London**
E	**Ecstasy**, a hallucinogenic drug
E	**Spain**, international vehicle registration
E	number of an EC-approved food additive, such as E111
ea.	**each**
EA	**enterprise allowance**
EAK	**Kenya**; international vehicle registration
EAN	*(Computing)* **European Academic Network**
E & OE	**errors and omissions excepted**; used on invoices
EAP	**English for academic purposes**
EARN	*(Computing)* **European Academic and Research Network**
EAROM	*(Computing)* **electrically alterable read-only memory**
EAT	**Tanzania**, international vehicle registration; also EAZ
EAU	**Uganda**, international vehicle registration
EAW	**Electrical Association for Women**
EAZ	**Tanzania**, international vehicle registration; also EAT
EB	**electricity board**
EBCDIC	*(Computing)* **extended binary-coded decimal-interchange code**
EBRD	**European Bank for Reconstruction and Development**
EBU	**European Broadcasting Union**, an organization of W European public and national broadcasters
EC	postcode for **east central London**
EC	**Ecuador**; international vehicle registration
EC	**European Community**, a political and economic alliance of European countries, which allows free movement of goods and capital. It is increasingly referred to as the European Union.

Eccl. *or*
Eccles. *(Bible)* **Ecclesiastes**
ECD **estimated completion date**
ECG **electrocardiogram** *or* **electrocardiograph**, a graphic recording of the electrical changes in the heart muscle, as detected by electrodes
ECM **electronic countermeasures**, jamming or otherwise rendering useless an opponent's radar, radio, television, etc.
ECOSOC **Economic and Social Council**, a United Nations institution
ECOWAS **Economic Community of West African States**, an organization established in 1975
ECR **electronic cash register**
ECS **European Communications Satellite**
ECSC **European Coal and Steel Community**
ECT **electroconvulsive therapy**, a controversial treatment for schizophrenia and depression
ECT *(Medicine)* **emission-computerized tomography**
ECTU **European Confederation of Trade Unions**
ecu *or* **ECU** **European Currency Unit**, the official monetary unit of the EC
ed. **edited**
ed. **edition**
ed. **editor**
ed. **education**
Ed. **Editor**
EDC **Economic Development Committee**
EDC **European Defence Community**
EDF **European Development Fund**
EDP **electronic data processing**
EDT *(US)* **Eastern Daylight Time**
EE **Early English**
EE **electrical engineer**
EE **errors excepted**
EEC **European Economic Community**, established in 1957 to create a single European market for the products of member states
EEG **electroencephalogram** *or* **electroencephalograph**, a graphic record of the electrical discharges of the brain, as detected by electrodes placed on the scalp

EEMS *(Computing)* **enhanced expanded memory specification**
EENT **ear, eye, nose, and throat**
EEPROM *(Computing)* **electrically erasable programmable read-only memory**, a memory that can record data and retain it indefinitely
EEROM *(Computing)* **electrically erasable read-only memory**
EET **Eastern European Time**
EETPU **Electrical, Electronic, Telecommunications, and Plumbing Union**
EFA **European Fighter Aircraft**
EFI **electronic fuel injection**
EFIS **electronic flight-information system**
EFL **English as a foreign language**
EFM *(Medicine)* **electronic fetal monitor**
EFT **electronic funds-transfer**
EFTA **European Free Trade Association**. Members are Austria, Finland, Iceland, Norway, Sweden, Switzerland, and Liechtenstein.
EFTPOS **electronic funds transfer at point of sale**, the transfer of funds from one bank account to another by electronic means
EFTS **electronic funds transfer system**
e.g. ***exempli gratia*** (Latin), for example
EGA *(Computing)* **enhanced graphics adapter**
EH postcode for **Edinburgh**
EHF **extremely high frequency**
EHO **Environmental Health Officer**
e.h.t. *or* **EHT** *(Electronics)* **extra-high tension**
EHV **extra-high voltage**
EIA **Engineering Industries Association**
EIA **exercise-induced asthma**
EIB **European Investment Bank**, an institution of the European Community, which finances capital investment
EIS *(Computing)* **executive information system**
EISA *(Computing)* **extended industry standard architecture**
EIU **Economic Intelligence Unit**
ELA **electronic learning aid**
elec. *or* **elect.** **electric, electrical, electricity** *or* **electronic**
elev. **elevation**

ELF **extremely low frequency**
ELISA *(Medicine)* **enzyme-linked immunosorbent assay**
ELT **English language teaching**
ELV **expendable launch vehicle**
em *or* **e.m.** *or* **EM** **electromagnetic**
EM **enlisted man** *or* **enlisted men**
EMA **European Monetary Agreement**
E-mail **electronic mail**, a system that enables the users of a computer network to send messages to other users
EMCOF **European Monetary Cooperative Fund**
EME **East Midlands Electricity**
emf *or* **e.m.f.** *(Physics)* **electromotive force**, the energy supplied by a source of electric power in driving a unit charge around an electrical circuit
EMI **Electric and Musical Industries**, a record company
Emp. **Emperor**
EMP **electromagnetic pulse**
EMR **electromagnetic radiation**
EMS **European Monetary System**, which aims to bring financial cooperation and monetary stability to the European Community
EMS *(Computing)* **expanded memory specification**
e.m.u. **electromagnetic unit**
EMU **economic and monetary union**, the proposed European Community policy for a single currency and common economic policies
EMU **electromagnetic unit**
EN postcode for **Enfield**
EN **Enrolled Nurse**
ENB **English National Ballet**
enc. *or* **encl.** **enclosed** *or* **enclosure**
ENE **east-northeast**
ENEA **European Nuclear Energy Agency**
eng. **engine**
eng. **engineer**
ENG **electronic news gathering**
EN(G) **Enrolled Nurse (General)**
EN(M) **Enrolled Nurse (Mental)**
EN(MH) **Enrolled Nurse (Mental Handicap)**

ENO	**English National Opera**
ENT	**ear, nose, and throat**, a hospital department or clinic
E-number	EC-approved code number of a food additive, such as E111
EO	**Equal Opportunities**
EO	**Executive Officer**
EOB	*(Computing)* **end of block**
EOC	**Equal Opportunities Commission**, established by the British government to implement the Sex Discrimination Act and prevent discrimination, particularly on sexual or marital grounds
EOD	*(Computing)* **end of data**
EOF	*(Computing)* **end of file**
EOJ	*(Computing)* **end of job**
EOQC	**European Organization for Quality Control**
EOT	*(Computing)* **end of tape**
EOT	*(Computing)* **end of transmission**
EP	**extended play** (record)
EPA	**Environmental Protection Agency**, a US agency set up to control water and air quality, industrial and commercial wastes, pesticides, noise, and traffic
EPCOT	**Experimental Prototype Community of Tomorrow**, a community in Florida
Eph. *or* **Ephes.**	*(Bible)* **Ephesians**
EPI	**Eysenck Personality Inventory** (test)
EPNS	**electroplated nickel silver**
EPOS	**electronic point of sale**
EPROM	*(Computing)* **erasable programmable read-only memory**
EPS	**European Passenger Services**, a transport company owned by British Rail
EPU	**European Payments Union**
eq.	**equal**
eq.	**equation**
eq. *or* **equiv.**	**equivalent**
Er	chemical symbol for **erbium**
ER	**Eduardus Rex** (Latin), King Edward
ER	**Elizabeth Regina** (Latin), Queen Elizabeth
ER	*(Medicine)* **emergency room**

ERA **Equal Rights Amendment**, referring to sexual and other equality under the US constitution
ERC **Economic Research Council**
ERC **Electronics Research Council**
ERDF **European Development Fund**
ERM **Exchange Rate Mechanism**, a voluntary system of semi-fixed exchange rates based on the European Currency Unit
ERNIE **electronic random number indicator equipment**, a machine that selects random numbers to indicate prizewinners in the British government's national lottery
ERV **English Revised Version**, of the Bible
ERW **enhanced radiation weapon**, also called the neutron bomb
Es chemical symbol for **einsteinium**
ES **El Salvador**, international vehicle registration
ESA **Environmentally Sensitive Area**, a scheme to protect beautiful areas of the British countryside from loss and damage caused by agricultural change
ESA **European Space Agency**
ESB **electrical stimulation of the brain**
ESCAP **Economic and Social Commission for Asia and the Pacific**, a United Nations agency
Esda **electrostatic deposition** (*or* **document**) **analysis**, a technique used for revealing indentations on paper, which helps determine whether documents have been tampered with
ESE **east-southeast**
ESF **European Science Foundation**
ESL **English as a second language**
ESN **educationally subnormal**
ESNS **educationally subnormal, serious**
ESOL **English for speakers of other languages**
ESOP **employee share-ownership plan**
esp. **especially**
ESP **English for specific purposes** *or* **English for special purposes**
ESP **extrasensory perception**
ESPRIT **European strategic programme for research and development in information technology**
Esq. **Esquire**; used in addressing letters

esr **electric sunroof**; used in car advertisements
ESRC **Economic and Social Research Council**
Ess **Essex**, an English county
est. **established**
est. **estimate** *or* **estimated**
Est. **established**
EST *(US)* **Eastern Standard Time**
EST **electric shock treatment** *or* **electroshock therapy**
Esth. *(Bible)* **Esther**
esu *or* **e.s.u.** *(Physics)* **electrostatic unit**
ESU **English-Speaking Union**, a society for promoting the fellowship of the English-speaking peoples of the world
E. Suss **East Sussex**, an English county
ET *(US)* **Eastern Time**
ET **Egypt**, international vehicle registration
ET **Employment Training**
ET **extraterrestrial**
Eta **Euzkadi ta Askatasuna**, Basque Nation and Liberty, a separatist organization
ETA **estimated time of arrival**
ETA **Euzkadi ta Askatasuna**, Basque Nation and Liberty, a separatist organization
et al. ***et alibii*** (Latin), and elsewhere
et al. ***et alii*** (Latin), and others; used in bibliographies
etc. ***et cetera*** (Latin), and other things
ETD **estimated time of departure**
ETD *(Telephony)* **extension trunk dialling**
ETF **electronic transfer of funds**
ETH **Ethiopia**, international vehicle registration
et seq. ***et sequens*** (Latin), and the following
ETUC **European Trade Union Confederation**
ETV *(US)* **educational television**
Eu chemical symbol for **europium**
EU **European Union**, the name by which the European Community is increasingly known
Euratom **European Atomic Energy Community**, which seeks cooperation in nuclear research and the development of nuclear energy
Eutelsat **European Telecommunications Satellite Organization**
EUV *(Physics)* **extreme ultraviolet**

EUW **European Union of Women**
EV **English Version**, of the Bible
EVA *(Astronautics)* **extravehicular activity**
EW **electronic warfare**
EW **enlisted woman** *or* **enlisted women**
e/windows **electric windows**; used in car advertisements
EWO **Educational Welfare Officer**
Ex. *(Bible)* **Exodus**
EX postcode for **Exeter**
ex lib. ***ex libris*** (Latin), from the library of; used on bookplates
Exod. *(Bible)* **Exodus**
expwy. *(US)* **expressway**
Ez. *(Bible)* **Ezra**
Ezek. *(Bible)* **Ezekiel**

F

f	*(Music)* ***forte*** (Italian), loudly
f.	**folio**
F	symbol for **farad**, a unit of electric capacitance
F	**fighter**; used on military aircraft, such as the F-061
F	chemical symbol for **fluorine**
F	**franc**, unit of currency
F	**France**, international vehicle registration
°F	symbol for **degrees Fahrenheit**
f.a. *or* **FA**	**Football Association**
FAA	*(US)* **Federal Aviation Agency**
FAA	**Film Artists' Association**
FAA	**Fleet Air Arm**
FAB	**fuel-air bomb**
FAE	**fuel-air explosive**, a warhead containing a highly flammable petroleum and oxygen mixture
f and f	**fixtures and fittings**
f.a.o.	**for the attention of**; used on letters
FAO	**Food and Agriculture Organization**, a United Nations agency concerned with improving nutrition and food and timber production throughout the world
FAS	*(Medicine)* **fetal alcohol syndrome**
fax *or* **FAX**	**facsimile transmission**
FBA	**Federation of British Artists**
FBI	**Federal Bureau of Investigation**, an agency of the US Department of Justice
FBL	**flight-by-light**, an aircraft control system
f.c.	*(Printing)* **follow copy**
FC	**Football Club**
fcap	**foolscap**, a size of writing or printing paper
FCB	*(Computing)* **file control block**
FCO	**Foreign and Commonwealth Office**
fcp	**foolscap**, a size of writing or printing paper
FCS	**Federation of Conservative Students**

FCU **fighter control unit**
f.d. **focal distance**
FD *(US)* **Fire Department**
FDA *(US)* **Food and Drug Administration**
FDF **Food and Drink Federation**
FDIC *(US)* **Federal Deposit Insurance Corporation**
FDP **Freie Demokratische Partei**, Free Democratic Party, a German liberal political party
FDR **Franklin Delano Roosevelt**, US president 1933–45
Fe chemical symbol for **iron**
FE further education
fec. ***fecit*** (Latin), he or she made it; used next to the artist's name on a work of art
Fed. **Federal**
FEL **free-electron laser**
fem. **female** *or* **feminine**
FEPC *(US)* **Fair Employment Practices Committee**
FET *(US)* **Federal Excise Tax**
FET **field-effect transistor**
ff **factory fitted**; used in car advertisements
ff ***fecerunt*** (Latin), they made it; used next to the artists' names on a work of art
ff **folios**
ff **the following** (pages)
ff *(Music)* ***fortissimo*** (Italian), very loudly
f.f. **fixed focus**
FF **Fianna Fáil** (Irish Gaelic), Warriors of Ireland, a moderate centre-right Irish political party
FF **form feed**; used on printers
fff *(Music)* ***fortississimo*** (Italian), as loudly as possible
FFF **Free French Forces**
FFHC **Freedom from Hunger Campaign**
FFPS **Fauna and Flora Preservation Society**
FG **Fine Gael** (Irish Gaelic), tribe of the Gaels, a moderate centre-left Irish political party
FHA *(US)* **Federal Housing Administration**
Fiat *or* **FIAT** **Fabbrica Italiana Automobili Torino**, an Italian car manufacturer based in Turin
FIDE **Fédération internationale des échecs** (French), International Chess Federation

FIFA	**Fédération internationale de football association** (French), International Federation of Association Football
fifo *or* **FIFO**	*(Computing, Accounting)* **first in first out**
fig.	**figurative**
fig.	**figure**
FILO	*(Computing, Accounting)* **first in last out**
FIMBRA	**Financial Intermediaries, Managers, and Brokers Regulatory Association**
f.i.o.	**for information only**
FIRA	**Furniture Industry Research Association**
FIS	**Family Income Supplement**
FJI	**Fiji**, international vehicle registration
FK	postcode for **Falkirk**
fl.	***floruit*** (Latin), he flourished or she flourished; used to indicate the period that someone was working when their birth and death dates are not known
FL	**Flight Lieutenant**
FL	postcode for **Florida**, a US state
FL	**Liechtenstein**, international vehicle registration
Fla.	**Florida**, a US state
flops *or* **FLOPS**	*(Computing)* **floating-point operations per second**
fl oz	**fluid ounce**
FLQ	**Front de Libération de Québec** (French), Quebec Liberation Front, a Canadian separatist group
Flt	**Flight**
F/Lt *or* **F.Lt**	**Flight Lieutenant**
Flt Cmdr	**Flight Commander**
Flt Lt	**Flight Lieutenant**
Flt Off.	**Flight Officer**
Flt Sgt	**Flight Sergeant**
f.m. *or* **Fm**	chemical symbol for **fermium**
FM	Field Marshal
FM	*(Physics)* **frequency modulation**, the method by which radio waves are altered for the transmission of broadcasting signals
FMB	**Federation of Master Builders**
FMCG	**fast-moving consumer goods**
FMD	**foot-and-mouth disease**, a contagious eruptive viral disease of cloven-hoofed animals

FMS **flight management systems**
FNLA **Front National de Libération de l'Angola** (French), National Front for the Liberation of Angola
fo. **folio**
FO **Field Officer**
FO **Flying Officer**
FO **Foreign Office**
FO *(Military)* **forward observer**
fob **free-on-board**, used to describe a valuation of goods at point of embarkation; export values are usually expressed fob for customs and excise purposes
FoC **father of the chapel**, a trade union office
FoE *or* **FOE** **Friends of the Earth, an environmental pressure group**
FOFA **follow-on forces attack**
FOIA *(US)* **Freedom of Information Act**
fol. **folio**
foll. **followed** *or* **following**
FOREST **Freedom Organization for the Right to Enjoy Smoking Tobacco**
Fortran *or* **FORTRAN** *(Computing)* **formula translation**, a programming language used especially in science
FOX **Futures and Options Exchange**
fp **foolscap**, a size of writing or printing paper
fp *(Music)* ***forte-piano*** (Italian), loud then soft
fp **freezing point**
FP **Fremskridtspartiet**, Progress Party, a Danish radical antibureaucratic political party
FPA **Family Planning Association**
FPC **Family Practitioner Committee**
FPC *(US)* **Federal Power Commission**
FPC **fish protein concentrate**
FPU *(Computing)* **floating point unit**
fps *or* **f.p.s.** **feet per second**
Fr chemical symbol for **francium**
Fr ***Frau*** (German), Mrs
FR **Faroe Islands**, international vehicle registration
FRAME **Fund for the Replacement of Animals in Medical Experiments**
FRB *(US)* **Federal Reserve Board**

FRG **Federal Republic of Germany**
Frl ***Fräulein*** (German), Miss
front. **frontispiece**
FRS **Federal Reserve System**, the US central banking system and note-issue authority
frt *or* **Frt** **freight**
frwy. *(US)* **freeway**
fsh **full service history**; used in car advertisements
FSH *(Medicine)* **follicle-stimulating hormone**, a hormone produced by the pituitary gland
FSLIC *(US)* **Federal Savings and Loan Insurance Corporation**
FSO **Foreign Service Officer**
ft **foot** *or* **feet**
FT **Financial Times**
FTA Index **Financial Times Actuaries Share Index**
FTAM *(Computing)* **file transfer, access, and management**
FTASI **Financial Times Actuaries All-Share Index**
FTAT **Furniture, Timber, and Allied Trades Union**, a British trade union
FTC **Federal Trade Commission**, the US anti-monopoly organization
FT Index **Financial Times Index**, an indicator measuring the daily movement of 30 major industrial share prices on the London Stock Exchange
FT Ord **Financial Times (Industrial) Ordinary Share Index**
ft/s **feet per second**
FTSE 100 *or* **FT-SE 100** **Financial Times Stock Exchange 100 Index**, known as Footsie
FTZ **free-trade zone**
fwd **forward**
f.w.d. **four-wheel drive**
f.w.d. **front-wheel drive**
f.w.t. *or* **FWT** **fair wear and tear**
FY postcode for **Blackpool**
FY fiscal year
FYC Family and Youth Concern
f.y.i. *or* **FYI** **for your information**

G

g	**gallon** *or* **gallons**
g	symbol for **gram**, a unit of weight
G	**$1000** *or* **£1000** (slang)
G	**general exhibition**, a US film classification
G	postcode for **Glasgow**
G3	**Group of Three**, the three most powerful economies in the world
G7	**Group of Seven**, the world's seven wealthiest nations: the US, Japan, Germany, France, the UK, Italy, and Canada
G24	**Group of Twenty-Four** (industrialized nations)
G77	**Group of Seventy-Seven** (developing countries)
Ga	chemical symbol for **gallium**
Ga.	**Georgia**, a US state
GA	**Gamblers Anonymous**
GA	**General Assembly** (of the United Nations)
GA	*(US)* **General of the Army**
GA	postcode for **Georgia**, a US state
GAFTA	**Grain and Free Trade Association**
gal	**gallon**
Gal.	*(Bible)* **Galatians**
gall.	**gallon**
G & S	**Gilbert and Sullivan**
g and t *or* **G & T**	**gin and tonic**
GAO	*(US)* **General Accounting Office**
GAR	**Grand Army of the Republic**, in the American Civil War
Gatt *or* **GATT**	**General Agreement on Tariffs and Trade**, an organization which encourages free trade between nations
GAW	*(US)* **guaranteed annual wage**
GB	**Great Britain**, international vehicle registration
GBA	**Alderney**, international vehicle registration
GBE	**Grand Cross of the Order of the British Empire**

GBG **Guernsey**, international vehicle registration
GBH **grievous bodily harm**, serious physical damage suffered by the victim of a crime
GBJ **Jersey**, international vehicle registration
GBM **Isle of Man**, international vehicle registration
GBS **George Bernard Shaw**, Irish dramatist and critic (1856–1950)
GBZ **Gibraltar**, international vehicle registration
GC **George Cross**, the highest British award to civilians for acts of courage in circumstances of great danger
GCA **ground-controlled approach**
GCA **Guatemala**, international vehicle registration
GCB **Grand Cross of the Order of the Bath**
GCC **Gas Consumers Council**
GCC **Gulf Cooperation Council**
GCE **General Certificate of Education**, an examination taken in Britain at the age of 16 (O level) and 18 (A level). O levels were replaced by the GCSE in 1988.
GCH **Grand Cross of the Hanoverian Order**
GCHQ **Government Communications Headquarters**, the centre of the British government's electronic surveillance operations, in Cheltenham, Gloucestershire
GCI **ground-controlled interception**
GCIE **Grand Commander of the Order of the Indian Empire**
GCLH **Grand Cross of the Legion of Honour**
GCLJ **Grand Cross of St Lazarus of Jerusalem**
GCM **Good Conduct Medal**
GCMG **Grand Cross of the Order of St Michael and St George**
GCON **Grand Cross of the Order of the Niger**
GCSE **General Certificate of Secondary Education**, an examination for 16-year-old pupils in Britain
GCSG **Grand Cross of the Order of St Gregory the Great**
GCSI **Grand Commander of the Order of the Star of India**
GCSJ **Grand Cross of Justice of the Order of St John of Jerusalem**
GCStJ **Grand Cross of the Most Venerable Order of the Hospital of St John of Jerusalem**
GCT **Greenwich Civil Time**
GCVO **Grand Cross of the Royal Victorian Order**
Gd chemical symbol for **gadolinium**

GD	**Grand Duchess**
GD	**Grand Duke**
GDBA	**Guide Dogs for the Blind Association**
GDC	**General Dental Council**
Gdns	**Gardens**; used in street names
GDP	**Gross Domestic Product**, the value of the output of all goods and services produced within a nation's borders
GDR	**German Democratic Republic**, the former state of East Germany
Ge	chemical symbol for **germanium**
GEC	**General Electric Company**
GEF	**Global Environmental Facility**, a part of the World Bank
gen.	*(Grammar)* **genitive**
Gen.	**General**
Gen.	*(Bible)* **Genesis**
ger.	*(Grammar)* **gerund**
Gerbil	**Great Education Reform Bill**, a British bill of 1988
Gestapo	***Geheime Staatspolizei***, Nazi Germany's secret police
GFR	**German Federal Republic**
GG	**Girl Guides**
GG	**Governor General**
gge	**garage**
GH	**Ghana**, international vehicle registration
GH	*(Medicine)* **growth hormone**
GHQ	*(Military)* **General Headquarters**
GI	**government issue**, hence a member or former member of the US armed forces
Gib.	**Gibraltar**
GIFT	*(Medicine)* **gamete intrafallopian transfer**, a form of fertility treatment
gigo *or* GIGO	*(Computing)* **garbage in, garbage out**
GINO	*(Computing)* **graphical input output**
Gk	**Greek**
GL	postcode for **Gloucester**
GL	**Grand Luxe**; used on car model numbers, e.g. Ford Escort 1.3 GL
GLAB	**Greater London Arts Board**
GLC	**Greater London Council**, the local authority that governed London 1965–86

GLCM	**ground-launched cruise missile**
Glos	**Gloucestershire**, an English county
GLR	**Greater London Radio**
gm	**gram**
GM	**general manager**
GM	**General Motors**, a US car manufacturer
GM	**George Medal**, a British civilian award for acts of great courage
GM	**grant-maintained** (school)
GM	**guided missile**
G-man	an FBI agent
GMB	**General, Municipal, Boilermakers**, a British trade union
GMB	**Grand Master of the Order of the Bath**
GMBE	**Grand Master of the Order of the British Empire**
GmbH	**Gesellschaft mit beschrankter Haftung** (German), limited liability company
GMC	**General Medical Council**
GMIE	**Grand Master of the Order of the Indian Empire**
GMKP	**Grand Master of the Knights of St Patrick**
GMMG	**Grand Master of the Order of St Michael and St George**
GMP	**Grand Master of the Order of St Patrick**
GMS	**grant-maintained status**, of a British school that has withdrawn from local authority support and is maintained directly by central government
GMSI	**Grand Master of the Order of the Star of India**
GMST	**Greenwich Mean Sidereal Time**
GMT	**Greenwich Mean Time**
GNP	**Gross National Product**, the most commonly used measurement of the wealth of a country
Gnr	**Gunner**
GNVQ	**General National Vocational Qualification**
GO	**General Office** *or* **General Officer**
GO	*(Military)* **general order**
GOM	**Grand Old Man**
GOP	**Grand Old Party** (the US Republican Party)
Gov.	**Governor**
govt *or* Govt	**government**
gox *or* GOX	**gaseous oxygen**
GP	**general practitioner**

GPALS **Global Protection Against Limited Strikes**, part of the Strategic Defense Initiative
Gp Capt **Group Captain**
gpd *or* **GPD** **gallons per day**
gph *or* **GPH** **gallons per hour**
gpm *or* **GPM** **gallons per minute**
GPMU **Graphical, Paper, and Media Union**, a British trade union
GPO **General Post Office**
GPO *(US)* **Government Printing Office**
GPR **ground-penetrating radar**
gps *or* **GPS** **gallons per second**
GPU **General Postal Union**; former name of the Universal Postal Union, a United Nations agency
GPU **Gosudarstvennoye Polititcheskoye Upravleniye** (Russian), State Political Administration, the former name for the KGB, the Soviet security service
GQ *(Military)* **general quarters**
Gr. **Greek**
GR ***Georgius Rex*** (Latin), King George
GR **Greece**, international vehicle registration
GRC **General Research Corporation**
grp **group**
GRP **glass-reinforced plastic**
GRT *(Medicine)* **gene replacement therapy**, hypothetical treatment for hereditary diseases in which affected cells would be removed, treated by genetic engineering, and the functioning cells reintroduced
GRU **Glavnoye Razvedyvatelnoye Upravleniye** (Russian), Central Intelligence Office
GS **General Secretary**
GS *(Military)* **General Staff**
GS **grammar school**
GSA **Girl Scouts of America**
GSA *(US)* **General Services Administration**
GSO **General Staff Officer**
gsoh *or* **GSOH** **good sense of humour**; used in newspaper lonely hearts advertisements
GSP **glass-fibre strengthened polyester**

GSS **Government Statistical Service**
GST **Greenwich Sidereal Time**
gt. ***gutta*** (Latin), a drop; used in prescriptions
GT **Gran Turismo** (Italian), grand touring; used on sports car model names, e.g. Citroën BX 19 GT
GTi **Gran Turismo Injection** (Italian); used on sports car model names, e.g. Peugeot 205 GTi
GTS **gas turbine ship**
g.u. *or* **GU** *(Medicine)* **genito-urinary**
GU **Guam**, an island in the W Pacific
GU postcode for **Guildford**
guar. **guarantee** *or* **guaranteed**
GUI *(Computing)* **graphic user-interface**, a type of interface in which programs and files appear as icons, which the operator can point at using a mouse
GUM **Gosudarstvenniy Universalni Magazin** (Russian), Universal State Store
GUT *(Physics)* **grand unified theory**, part of the programme seeking a unified field theory, which would combine all the forces of nature within one framework
GUY **Guyana**, international vehicle registration
GV ***grande vitesse*** (French), fast goods train
GW **guided weapons**
GWR **Great Western Railway**
Gy symbol for **gray**, a unit of absorbed radiation dose
gyn. *or* **gynaecol.** **gynaecological** *or* **gynaecology**
Gy. Sgt. **Gunnery Sergeant**

H

h.	**height**
h.	*(Baseball)* **hit** *or* **hits**
H	**hard**; used on pencils
H	symbol for **henry**, a unit of inductance
H	**heroin** (slang)
H	**hospital**; used on signs
H	**Hungary**; international vehicle registration
H	chemical symbol for **hydrogen**
ha	symbol for **hectare**
HA	postcode for **Harrow**
HA	**Health Authority**
HA	**heavy artillery**
HAA	**heavy anti-aircraft**
Hab.	*(Bible)* **Habakkuk**
Hag.	*(Bible)* **Haggai**
HAI	**hospital-acquired infection**
h & c *or* **H & C**	**hot and cold**
H. & W.	**Hereford and Worcester**, an English county
Hants	**Hampshire**, an English county
HAT	**housing action trust** *or* **housing association trust**
HB	**hard-black**; used on pencils
HBIG	*(Medicine)* **hepatitis B immunoglobulin**
HBLV	*(Medicine)* **human B-lymphotropic virus**
HBM	**Her/His Britannic Majesty**
H-bomb	**hydrogen bomb**
HBP	*(Medicine)* **high blood pressure**
HBV	*(Medicine)* **hepatitis B virus**
h.c.	***honoris causa*** (Latin), for the sake of honour
HC	**Holy Communion**
HC	**House of Commons**
HCAAS	**Homeless Children's Aid and Adoption Society**
hcap	**handicap**

HCFC	**hydrochlorofluorocarbon**
HCI	**human-computer interface** *or* **human-computer interaction**
hcl	**high cost of living**
hcp	**handicap**
HD	**Hodgkin's disease**
HD	postcode for **Huddersfield**
hdbk	**handbook**
HDD	*(Aeronatics, Computing)* **head-down display**
HDL	**high-density lipoprotein**
HDLC	*(Computing)* **high-level data link control**
hdqrs	**headquarters**
HDTV	**high-definition television**, a television system offering a significantly greater number of scanning lines, and therefore a clearer picture
hdw	**hardware**
He	chemical symbol for **helium**
HE	**higher education**
HE	**high explosive**
HE	**His Eminence**
HE	**Her/His Excellency**
Heb.	*(Bible)* **Hebrews**
HEO	**Higher Executive Officer**
HEOS	**high-elliptic-inclined-orbit satellite**
Herts	**Hertfordshire**, an English county
Hf	chemical symbol for **hafnium**
HF	**hard firm**; used on pencils
HF	*(Physics)* **high frequency**
HFC	*(Electricity)* **high-frequency current**
HFC	**hydrofluorocarbon**
Hg	chemical symbol for **mercury**
HG	postcode for **Harrogate**
HGH	*(Medicine)* **human growth hormone**
HGV	**heavy goods vehicle**
HGW	**heat-generating waste**
hgwy	**highway**
HH	**Her/His Highness**
HH	**His Holiness**
HI	postcode for **Hawaii**, a US state
HI	***hic iacet*** (Latin), here lies

hi-fi **high fidelity**
HIH **Her/His Imperial Highness**
hilac *or* HILAC **heavy-ion linear accelerator**
HIM **Her/His Imperial Majesty**
HIS ***hic iacet sepultus or hic iacet sepulta*** (Latin), here lies buried
HIV **human immunodeficiency virus**, the virus that is transmitted in body fluids and causes AIDS
HJ ***hic jacet*** (Latin), here lies
HJS ***hic jacet sepultus or hic jacet sepulta*** (Latin), here lies buried
HK **Hong Kong**, international vehicle registration
HKJ **Jordan**, international vehicle registration
hl **hectolitre**
HL **House of Lords**
HLA *(Medicine)* **human lymphocyte antigen**
HLW **high-level (radioactive) waste**
hm **hectometre**
HM **hazardous material**
HM **headmaster** *or* **headmistress**
HM **Her/His Majesty**
HMA **Head Masters' Association**
HMA *(Computing)* **high-memory area**
HMCA **Hospital and Medical Care Association**
HMF **Her/His Majesty's Forces**
HMG **Her/His Majesty's Government**
HMI **Her/His Majesty's Inspector** (of schools)
HMI *(Computing)* **human-machine interface**
HMO *(US)* **health maintenance organization**
HMP ***hoc monumentum posuit*** (Latin), he or she erected this monument
HMS **Her/His Majesty's Service**
HMS **Her/His Majesty's Ship**
HMSO **Her/His Majesty's Stationery Office**, a British government department responsible for the production and sale of government publications
HMV **His Master's Voice**, a record company
HNC **Higher National Certificate**
HND **Higher National Diploma**

ho. **house**
Ho chemical symbol for **holmium**
HO **head office**
HO **Home Office**
HoC **House of Commons**
HoD **head of department**
H of C **House of Commons**
H of L **House of Lords**
H of R *(US)* **House of Representatives**
Hon. **Honorary** *or* **Honourable**; used in titles
hons **honours**
Hon. Sec. **Honorary Secretary**
HOOD *(Computing)* **hierarchical object-oriented design**
Hos. *(Bible)* **Hosea**
hosp. **hospital**
hp **horsepower**
h.p. *or* **HP** **hire purchase**
HP postcode for **Hemel Hempstead**
HP **Hewlett Packard**, a US electronics and computer company
HP **Houses of Parliament**
HPV *(Medicine)* **human papilloma virus**
HQ **headquarters**
hr **hour**
Hr ***Herr*** (German), Mr *or* Sir
HR postcode for **Hereford**
HR *(US)* **House of Representatives**
HRE **Holy Roman Emperor** *or* **Holy Roman Empire**
HRH **Her/His Royal Highness**
HRIP ***hic requiescit in pace*** (Latin), here rests in peace
HRP *(Military)* **human remains pouch**
hrs **hours**
HRT **hormone replacement therapy**, the use of oestrogen and progestogen to help limit the effects of the menopause in women
hrw **heated rear window**; used in car advertisements
HS ***hic sepultus*** *or* ***hic sepulta*** (Latin), here is buried
HS **High School**
HSA **human serum albumin**
HSC **Health and Safety Commission**
HSDU **hospital sterilization and disinfection unit**

HSE **Health and Safety Executive**
HSE ***hic sepultus est or hic sepulta est*** (Latin), here lies buried
HSH **Her/His Serene Highness**
HSI *(Computing)* **human-system interface** *or* **human-system interaction**
HSM **Her/His Serene Majesty**
HSSU **hospital sterile supply unit**
HST **Hawaiian Standard Time**
HST **high-speed train**
HST **hypersonic transport**
HSV *(Medicine)* **herpes simplex virus**
ht **height**
HT **Hawaii Time**
HTLV *(Medicine)* **human T-cell lymphotropic virus**
HTV **Harlech Television**, a television company
HU postcode for **Hull**
HUAC **House** (of Representatives) **Un-American Activities Committee**, a congressional committee established in 1938, noted for its public investigating into alleged subversion, particularly by communists, in the 1950s
HUD *(Aeronautics, Computing)* **head-up display**
HUD *(US)* **Department of Housing and Urban Development**
Hugo **Human Genome Organization**
HUMINT *(Military)* **human intelligence**
HUMV *(Military)* **human light vehicle**
Husat **Human Science and Advanced Technology ResearchInstitute**
h.v. **high velocity**
HV **health visitor**
HV **high velocity**
HV **high voltage**
HVAC **heating, ventilation, air conditioning**
HVAC **(Physics) high-voltage alternating current**
HVDC *(Physics)* **high-voltage direct current**
HVP **hydrolysed vegetable protein**
h.w. *(Cricket)* **hit wicket**
HW **hazardous waste**
hwy. *(US)* **highway**
HX postcode for **Halifax**
Hz symbol for **hertz**, a unit of frequency

I

i.	*(Grammar)* **intransitive**
I	chemical symbol for **iodine**
I	**Interstate (highway)**; used on US road numbers, e.g. the I5
I	**Italy**, international vehicle registration
I	Roman numeral for **1**
Ia	**Iowa**, a US state
IA	postcode for **Iowa**, a US state
IAA	**International Advertising Association**
IAAF	**International Amateur Athletic Federation**
IAAS	**Incorporated Association of Architects and Surveyors**
IAC	**Institute of Amateur Cinematographers**
IACP	**International Association of Chiefs of Police**
IADB	**Inter-American Development Bank**
IADR	**International Association for Dental Research**
IAEA	**International Atomic Energy Agency**, a United Nations agency that advises and assists member countries in the development and application of nuclear power
IAGB & I	**Ileostomy Association of Great Britain and Ireland**
IAHM	**Incorporated Association of Headmasters**
IALA	**International Association of Lighthouse Authorities**
IAM	**Institute of Administrative Management**
IAM	**Institute of Advanced Motorists**
IAO	**Incorporated Association of Organists**
IAPS	**Incorporated Association of Preparatory Schools**
IARF	**International Association for Religious Freedom**
IARU	**International Amateur Radio Union**
i.a.s.	**indicated air speed**
IAS	*(Computing)* **immediate access store**
IAS	**indicated air speed**
IAT	**International Atomic Time**
IATA	**International Air Transport Association**
IAU	**International Association of Universities**

IAU **International Astronomical Union**
IAWPRC **International Association on Water Pollution Research and Control**
IBA **Independent Broadcasting Authority**, the former name of the Independent Television Commission
IBA **International Bar Association**
IBBR **interbank bid rate**
IBF **International Badminton Federation**
IBF **International Boxing Federation**
IBG **Institute of British Geographers**
ibid. ***ibidem*** (Latin), in the same place; used in reference citations
IBiol **Institute of Biology**
IBM **International Business Machines Corporation**, a multinational computer company
IBMBR **interbank market bid rate**
IBRD **International Bank for Reconstruction and Development**, an agency of the United Nations that provides funds and technical assistance to help the poorer countries of the world. It is also known as the World Bank.
IBRO **International Bank Research Organization**
IBRO **International Brain Research Organization**
IBTE **Institution of British Telecommunications Engineers**
i/c **in charge (of)** *or* **in command (of)**
IC ***Iesus Christus*** (Latin), Jesus Christ
IC **integrated circuit**
ICA **Institute of Chartered Accountants**
ICA **Institute of Contemporary Arts**
ICA **International Cyclist Association**
ICAA **Invalid Children's Aid Association**
ICAEW **Institute of Chartered Accountants in England and Wales**
ICAO **International Civil Aviation Organization**, a United Nations agency that regulates safety and efficiency and air law
ICBM **intercontinental ballistic missile**
ICBN **International Code of Botanical Nomenclature**
ICBP **International Council for Bird Preservation**
ICC **International Chamber of Commerce**
ICC **International Cricket Conference**

ICC *(US)* **Interstate Commerce Commission**
ICCH **International Commodities Clearing House**
ICCPR **International Covenant on Civil and Political Rights** (of the UN)
ICE **Institution of Civil Engineers**
ICED **International Council for Educational Development**
ICEF **International Federation of Chemical, Energy, and General Workers' Unions**
ICES **International Council for the Exploration of the Sea**
ICF *(Nuclear engineering)* **inertial-confinement fusion**
ICF **International Canoe Federation**
ICFTU **International Confederation of Free Trade Unions**
IChemE **Institution of Chemical Engineers**
ICI **Imperial Chemical Industries**, one of Britain's largest companies, engaged in the manufacture and research of products and processes including agrochemicals, polymers, and electronics
ICJ **International Court of Justice**, the main judicial organ of the United Nations
ICL **International Computers Ltd**
ICM **Institute for Complementary Medicine**
ICM **Institute of Credit Management**
ICM **International Confederation of Midwives**
ICN **International Council of Nurses**
ICNB **International Code of Nomenclature of Bacteria**
ICNCP **International Code of Nomenclature of Cultivated Plants**
ICNV **International Code of Nomenclature of Viruses**
ICO **Islamic Conference Organization**, an association of 44 states in the Middle East, Africa, and Asia, which aims to promote Islamic solidarity and cooperation between member countries
ICOM **International Council of Museums**
ICOMOS **International Council of Monuments and Sites**
ICPO **International Criminal Police Organization**, known as Interpol
ICR *(Computing)* **intelligent character recognition**
ICRC **International Committee of the Red Cross**
ICRF **Imperial Cancer Research Fund**
ICRP **International Commission on Radiological Protection**

ICRU **International Commission on Radiation Units** (and Measurements)
ICS **International Chamber of Shipping**
ICS **investors' compensation scheme**
ICSA **Institute of Chartered Secretaries and Administrators**
ICSH *(Medicine)* **intrastitial-cell-stimulating hormone**
ICSI **intracytoplasmic sperm injection**, a method of in vitro fertilization that involves injecting a sperm into the centre of an egg
ICSLS **International Convention for Safety of Life at Sea**
ICU **intensive care unit**
ICW **International Congress of Women**
ICWA **Institute of Cost and Works Accountants**
ICZN **International Code of Zoological Nomenclature**
id. ***idem*** (Latin), the same
i.d. **inside diameter**
i.d. **intradermal**
Id. **Idaho**, a US state
ID postcode for **Idaho**, a US state
ID **identification**
ID **inside diameter**
ID **intradermal**
IDA **International Development Association**, a United Nations agency affiliated to the World Bank
IDD **insulin-dependent diabetes**
IDD *(Telephony)* **international direct dialling**
IDDD *(Telephony)* **international direct distance dial(ling)**
IDDM **insulin-dependent diabetes mellitus**
IDF **ınternational Dental Federation**
IDL **International Date Line**, a modification of the 180th meridian that marks the difference in time between east and west
IDMS *(Computing)* **integrated data-management system**
IDP *(Computing)* **integrated data processing**
IDP **International Driving Permit**
i.e. ***id est*** (Latin), that is
IEA **Institute of Economic Affairs**
IEA **International Energy Agency**
IEE **Institution of Electrical Engineers**

IEEE **Institute of Electrical and Electronic Engineers**, a US institute that sets technical standards for electrical equipment and computer data exchange
IEHO **Institution of Environmental Health Officers**
IEME **Inspectorate of Electrical and Mechanical Engineering**
IERE **Institution of Electronic and Radio Engineers**
IExpE **Institute of Explosives Engineers**
IF *(Electronics)* **intermediate frequency**
IFAD **International Fund for Agricultural Development**, a United Nations agency
IFALPA **International Federation of Air Line Pilots' Association**
IFAW **International Fund for Animal Welfare**
IFC **International Finance Corporation**
IFE *(Computing)* **intelligent front end**
iff *(Logic, Maths)* **if and only if**
IFGO **International Federation of Gynaecology and Obstetrics**
IFIP **International Federation for Information Processing**
IFL **International Friendship League**
IFLA **International Federation of Library Associations**
IFMC **International Folk Music Council**
IFP **Inkatha Freedom Party**, a South African political organization that aims to create a nonracial democratic political situation in the country
IFPI **International Federation of the Phonographic Industry**
IFR **instrument flying regulations**
IFRB **International Frequency Registration Board**
IFS **International Federation of Surveyors**
Ig *(Medicine)* **immunoglobulin**
IG postcode for **Ilford**
IGasE **Institution of Gas Engineers**
IGF *(Medicine)* **insulin-like growth factor**
IGM *(Chess)* **International Grandmaster**
IGS **independent grammar school**
IGU **International Gas Union**
IGU **International Geographical Union**
IGY **International Geophysical Year**
IH ***iacet hic*** (Latin), here lies
IHD **ischaemic heart disease**, a disorder caused by reduced perfusion of the coronary arteries due to atherosclerosis, the commonest cause of death in the western world

IHF	**International Hospitals Federation**
IHP	**indicated horsepower**
IHS	ΙΗΣΟΥΣ (Greek), Jesus; used as a monogram or symbol
IHSM	**Institute of Health Services Management**
IHT	**Institution of Highways and Transportation**
IIAC	**Industrial Injuries Advisory Council**
IIAS	**International Institute of Administrative Sciences**
IID	**insulin-independent diabetes**
IIM	**Institute of Industrial Managers**
IInfSc	**Institute of Information Scientists**
IIS	**International Institute of Sociology**
IKBS	*(Computing)* **intelligent knowledge-based system**
IL	postcode for **Illinois**, a US state
IL	**Institute of Linguists**
IL	**Israel**, international vehicle registration
ILA	**International Law Association**
ILC	**International Law Commission**, a United Nations body
ILEA	**Inner London Education Authority**, the authority that administered education in London until 1990
ILGWU	**International Ladies Garment Workers' Union**
ill.	**illustrated** *or* illustration
Ill.	**Illinois**, a US state
illus.	**illustrated** *or* **illustration**
ILO	**International Labour Organization**, part of the United Nations, which formulates standards for labour and social conditions
ILP	**Independent Labour Party**, a British socialist party founded in 1893, which no longer exists
ILR	**independent local radio**
ILS	**instrument landing system**
ILTF	**International Lawn Tennis Federation**
ILW	*(Nuclear engineering)* **intermediate-level waste**
i.m.	**intramuscular**
IM	*(Chess) International Master*
IM	**intramuscular**
IMA	**International Music Association**
IMarE	**Institute of Marine Engineers**
Imarsat *or* **IMARSAT**	**International Maritime Satellite Organization**
IMC	**Institute of Management Consultants**

IMC *(Aeronautics)* **instrument meteorological conditions**
IMCO **Intergovernmental Maritime Consultative Organization**, a United Nations body
IMEA **Incorporated Municipal Electrical Association**
IMechE **Institution of Mechanical Engineers**
IMF **International Monetary Fund**, an agency of the United Nations that promotes international monetary cooperation and world trade
IMinE **Institution of Mining Engineers**
Imint *or* **IMINT** *(Military)* **image intelligence**
IMM **Institute of Mining and Metallurgy**
IMO **International Maritime Organization**, an agency of the United Nations that promotes cooperation between governments on technical matters affecting merchant shipping
IMO **International Meteorological Organization**
IMO **International Miners' Organization**
IMRO **Investment Management Regulatory Organization**
IMS *(Computing)* (trademark) **Information Management System**
IMS **Institute of Management Services**
IMU **International Mathematical Union**
IMW **Institute of Masters of Wine**
in **inch**
In chemical symbol for **indium**
IN postcode for **Indiana**, a US state
INAO **Institut national des appellations d'origine des vins et eaux-de-vie** (French), the body controlling wine production
Inbucon **International Business Consultants**
Inc. **Incorporated**; used after US business names
INCA **International Newspaper Colour Association**
INCB **International Narcotics Control Board**, a United Nations agency
INCPEN **Industry Committee for Packaging and the Environment**
Ind. **Independent**
Ind. **Indiana**, a US state
IND **India**, international vehicle registration
INF **intermediate nuclear forces**

INLA **Irish National Liberation Army**, a guerrilla organization committed to the end of British rule in Northern Ireland and the incorporation of Ulster into the Irish Republic
INR **independent national radio**
INRI ***Iesus Nazarenus Rex Iudaeorum*** (Latin), Jesus of Nazareth, King of the Jews
Ins **insert**; used on a keyboard
INS **International News Service**
Inset *or* **INSET** **in-service training**
inst. **instant** (this month)
Inst. **institute** *or* **institution**
InstAct **Institute of Actuaries**
InstBE **Institution of British Engineers**
InstE **Institute of Energy**
InstMM **Institution of Mining and Metallurgy**
InstP **Institute of Physics**
InstPet **Institute of Petroleum**
InstPI **Institute of Patentees and Inventors**
InstR **Institute of Refrigeration**
InstSMM **Institute of Sales and Marketing Management**
InstT **Institute of Transport**
Intelsat *or* **INTELSAT** **International Telecommunications Satellite Consortium**
Interpol **International Criminal Police Organization**, an agency that has an international criminal register, fingerprint file, and methods index
INucE **Institution of Nuclear Engineers**
IO **intelligence officer**
I/O **inboard/outboard** (motorboat engine)
I/O *(Computing)* **input/output**
IOC **International Olympic Committee**
IOCU **International Organization of Consumers' Unions**
IoD **Institute of Directors**
IOF **Independent Order of Foresters**
I of E **Institute of Export**
IoJ **Institute of Journalists**
IOM **Isle of Man**
IOOF **Independent Order of Oddfellows**, a friendly society of

18th-century origin
IOP *(Computing)* **input/output processor**
Iosco *or*
IOSCO **International Organization of Securities Commissions**
IOU **I owe you**, a written acknowledgment of debt
IOW **Isle of Wight**, an English county
IP *(Baseball)* **Innings pitched**
IP postcode for **Ipswich**
IPA **Institute of Practitioners in Advertising**
IPA **International Phonetic Alphabet**
IPA **International Phonetic Association**
IPA **International Publishers' Association**
IPC **International Polar Commission**
IPC **International Publishing Corporation**
IPCC **Intergovernmental Panel on Climatic Change**, a United Nations body
IPCS **Institution of Professional Civil Servants**
IPE **Institution of Plant Engineers**
IPE **Institution of Production Engineers**
IPE **International Petroleum Exchange**
IPFA **Institute of Public Finance and Accountancy**
IPI **Institute of Patentees and Inventors**
IPI **International Press Institute**
IPlantE **Institution of Plant Engineers**
IPM **Institute of Personnel Management**
IPPA **Independent Programme Producers' Association**
IPPF **International Planned Parenthood Federation**
IPPR **Institute for Public Policy Research**
IPPS **Institute of Physics and the Physical Society**
IPR **Institute of Public Relations**
IProdE **Institute of Production Engineers**
ips **inches per second**
ips *(Computing)* **instructions per second**
IPS **Institute of Purchasing and Supply**
IPT **Institute of Petroleum Technologists**
IPTS **International Practical Temperature Scale**
IPU **Inter-Parliamentary Union**
IQ **Intelligence Quotient**, the ratio between a subject's mental and chronological ages, multiplied by 100
IQA **Institute of Quality Assurance**

IQS **Institute of Quantity Surveyors**
ir *(Physics)* **infrared**
Ir chemical symbol for **iridium**
IR **information retrieval**
IR *(Physics)* **infrared**
IR **Inland Revenue**
IR **Iran**, international vehicle registration
IRA **Irish Republican Army**, a militant Irish nationalist organization whose aim is to create a united Irish socialist republic including Ulster, using force to try to achieve its objectives
IRAD **Institute for Research on Animal Diseases**
IRBM **intermediate-range ballistic missile**
IRF **International Rowing Federation**
IRFB **International Rugby Football Board**
Iris **infrared intruder system**
IRIS **International Research and Information Service**
IRL **Republic of Ireland**, international vehicle registration
IRN **Independent Radio News**
IRO **Inland Revenue Office**
IRO **International Refugee Organization**
IRPA **International Radiation Protection Association**
IRQ *(Computing)* **interrupt request**
IRQ **Iraq**, international vehicle registration
IRRI **International Rice Research Institute**
IRRV **Institute of Revenues, Rating and Valuation**
IRS *(US)* **Internal Revenue Service**
IRTE **Institute of Road Transport Engineers**
Is. *(Bible)* **Isaiah**
IS **Iceland**, international vehicle registration
Isa *(Bible)* **Isaiah**
ISA **International Sociological Association**
ISA *(Aeronautics)* **International Standard Atmosphere**
ISAM *(Computing)* **indexed sequential access method**
ISBA **Incorporated Society of British Advertisers**
ISBN **International Standard Book Number**; used for ordering or classifying book titles
ISCE **International Society of Christian Endeavour**
ISCh **Incorporated Society of Chiropodists**
ISCM **International Society for Contemporary Music**

ISCO **Independent Schools Careers Organization**
ISD *(Telephony)* **international subscriber dialling**
ISDN **Integrated Services Digital Network**, an internationally developed telecommunications system for sending signals in digital format along optical fibres and coaxial cable
ISE **Institution of Structural Engineers**
ISF **International Shipping Federation**
ISI **International Statistical Institute**
ISI **Iron and Steel Institute**
ISIS **Independent Schools Information Service**
ISJC **Independent Schools Joint Council**
ISM **Incorporated Society of Musicians**
ISMRC **Inter-Services Metallurgical Research Council**
ISO **Imperial Service Order**
ISO **International Standards Organization**, set up to standardize technical terms, specifications, units, and so on
ISO *(Photography)* a numbering system for rating the speed of films, designed by the International Standards Organization
ISP **Institute of Sales Promotion**
ISP **International Study Programme**
ISPEMA **Industrial Safety (Personal Equipment) Manufacturers' Association**
ISR **information storage and retrieval**
ISRO **International Securities Regulatory Organization**
ISSN **International Standard Serial Number**
IST **Institute of Science Technology**
ISTC **Institute of Scientific and Technical Communicators**
ISTC **Iron and Steel Trades' Confederation**
ISTD **Imperial Society of Teachers of Dancing**
IStructE **Institution of Structural Engineers**
ISU **International Seamen's Union**
ISV **International Scientific Vocabulary**
ISVA **Incorporated Society of Valuers and Auctioneers**
IT **information technology**, the use of computers to produce, store, handle, and retrieve information
IT *(Physics)* **International Table**
ita **Independent Television Authority**, a body superseded by the IBA
ITA **initial teaching alphabet**

ITA	**Independent Television Authority**, a body superseded by the IBA
ITAI	**Institution of Technical Authors and Illustrators**
ital.	**italic**
ITAR-TASS	**Information Telegraph Agency of Russia**, Russian news service
ITB	**Industry Training Board**
ITB	**International Time Bureau**
ITC	**Independent Television Commission**, the British regulatory body for commercial television and radio
ITC	**International Tin Council**
ITC	**International Trade Centre**
ITE	**Institute of Terrestrial Ecology**
ITEME	**Institution of Technician Engineers in Mechanical Engineering**
ITF	**International Tennis Federation**
ITF	**International Trade Federations**
ITF	**International Transport Workers' Federation**
ITI	**Institute of Translating and Interpreting**
ITMA	**Institute of Trade Mark Agents**
ITMA	**It's That Man Again** (BBC radio programme)
ITN	*(UK)* **Independent Television News**
ITO	**International Trade Organization**
ITS	**Industrial Training Service**
ITS	**International Trade Secretariat**
ITT	**International Telephone and Telegraph Corporation**
ITTF	**International Table Tennis Federation**
ITU	**intensive therapy unit**
ITU	**International Telecommunications Union**, a United Nations agency that allocates radio frequencies and promotes low tariffs and life-saving measures for disasters at sea
ITU	**International Typographical Union**
ITV	*(UK)* **Independent Television**
ITV	*(US)* **instructional television**
IU	**Izquierda Unida**, United Left, a Spanish extreme left-wing political party
IUA	**International Union of Architects**
IUB	**International Union of Biochemistry**
IUCD	**intrauterine contraceptive device**

IUCN **International Union for Conservation of Nature**, established by the United Nations to promote the conservation of wildlife and habitats
IUCW **International Union for Child Welfare**
IUD **intrauterine device**, a method of contraception
IUGG **International Union of Geodesy and Geophysics**
IUGR **intrauterine growth retardation**
IUGS **International Union of Geological Sciences**
IUHPS **International Union of the History and Philosophy of Science**
IULA **International Union of Local Authorities**
IUMI **International Union of Marine Insurance**
IUPAC **International Union of Pure and Applied Chemistry**
IUPAP **International Union of Pure and Applied Physics**
IUPS **International Union of Physiological Sciences**
IUTAM **International Union of Theoretical and Applied Mechanics**
i.v. **intravenous**
IV **interactive video**, a computer-mediated system that enables the user to interact with and control information stored on video disc
IV **intravenous**
IV postcode for **Inverness**
IVF **in vitro fertilization**, a method of allowing eggs and sperm to unite in a laboratory to form embryos, which can then be implanted in the mother's womb
IVR **international vehicle registration**
IVS **International Voluntary Service**
IWA **Inland Waterways Association**
IWC **International Whaling Commission**
IWEM **Institution of Water and Environmental Management**
IWW **Industrial Workers of the World**, a labour movement dedicated to the overthrow of capitalism and the creation of a single union for workers
IWW **International Workers of the World**
IYRU **International Yacht Racing Union**

J

J **jack**; used on playing cards
J **Japan**, international vehicle registration
J symbol for **joule**, a unit of energy or work
JA **Jamaica**, international vehicle registration
JA *(US)* **Judge Advocate**
JA **Justice of Appeal**
Jaat *(Military)* **joint air attack team**
JACT **Joint Association of Classical Teachers**
JAG **Judge Advocate General**
JAL **Japan Airlines**
Jam. *(Bible)* **James**
JANET *(Computing)* **Joint Academic Network**
Jas. *(Bible)* **James**
JAT **Jugoslovenski Aero-Transport** , Yugoslav Airlines
jato *or* **JATO** **jet-assisted takeoff**, an aircraft takeoff using auxiliary rocket motors
JBCNS **Joint Board of Clinical Nursing Studies**
JC **Jesus Christ**
JC **Julius Caesar**
JCB an excavating machine, named after its manufacturer **Joseph Cyril Bamford**
JCC **Junior Chamber of Commerce**
JCI **Junior Chamber International**
JCL *(Computing)* **job-control language**
JCR **junior common room**, in a university
JCS **Joint Chiefs of Staff**
jct. *or* **jctn** **junction**
JCWI **Joint Council for the Welfare of Immigrants**
JD **juvenile delinquent**
JD *(US)* **Justice Department**
JDL *(US)* **Jewish Defense League**
Jer. *(Bible)* **Jeremiah**
JESSI **Joint European Submicron Silicon Initiative**

JET **Joint European Torus**, a machine to conduct experiments on nuclear fusion at Culham in Oxfordshire
JFET *(Electronics)* **junction field-effect transistor**
JFK **John Fitzgerald Kennedy**, US president 1961–63
jg *(US)* **junior grade**
JHS ***Jesus Hominum Salvator*** (Latin), Jesus Saviour of Men
jic **just in case**
JICTAR **Joint Industry Committee for Television Advertising Research**
jit *or* **JIT** **just-in-time**, a production management practice that can reduce expenses and improve efficiency
JJ **Judges**
JJ **Justices**
JMB **Joint Matriculation Board**, a British examination board
jn *or* **Jn** **junior**
Jn. *(Bible)* **John**
j.n.d. **just noticeable difference**
jnl *or* ***Jnl*** **journal**
jnr *or* **Jnr** **junior**
jnt **joint**
JO **joint officer**
Jon. *(Bible)* **Jonah**
Josh. *(Bible)* **Joshua**
JOVIAL *(Computing)* **Jules' own version of international algorithmic language**
JP **jet-propelled** *or* **jet propulsion**
JP **Justice of the Peace**
JPS **jet-propulsion system**
jr *or* **Jr** **junior**
JRC **Junior Red Cross**
JSB **joint-stock bank**
JSDC **Joint Service Defence College**
JSLS **Joint Services Liaison Staff**
JSSC **Joint Services Staff College**
J-stars **joint surveillance and targeting acquisition radar system**
jt **joint**
JTIDS **Joint Tactical Information Distribution Systems**
Jud. *or* **Judg.** *(Bible)* **Judges**
JUGFET *(Electronics)* **junction-gate field-effect transistor**

junc. *or* **Junc.**	**Junction**
JWV	**Jewish War Veterans**
JV	*(US)* **junior varsity**, a team of players who have failed to make the varsity; also written jayvee

K

k.	**karat**
k.	symbol for **kilogram**, a unit of weight
k.	**kitchen**
K	**Cambodia**; international vehicle registration
K	symbol for **kelvin**, a unit of temperature
K	*(Computing)* **kilobyte**
K	*(Chess)* **king**
K	**king**; used on playing cards
K	chemical symbol for **potassium**
K	**1000**
K9	*(Military)* **canine**
KA	postcode for **Kilmarnock**
Kan.	**Kansas**, a US state
k & b	**kitchen and bathroom**
Kans.	**Kansas**, a US state
Kb *or* **KB**	*(Computing)* **kilobyte**
KB	**Knight Bachelor**
KB	*(Computing)* **knowledge base**
kbd	**keyboard**
KBE	**Knight Commander of the Order of the British Empire**
KBS	**Knight of the Blessed Sacrament**
KBS	*(Computing)* **knowledge-based system**, a program that uses an encoding of human knowledge to help solve problems
kbyte	**kilobyte**
kc	**kilocycle**
KC	**King's Counsel**
KC	**Knight Commander**
KC	**Knights of Columbus**
kcal	**kilocalorie**
KCB	**Knight Commander of the Order of the Bath**
K cell	*(Medicine)* **killer cell**
KCH	**King's College Hospital**, in London

KCH — **Knight Commander of the Hanoverian Order**
KCHS — **Knight Commander of the Order of the Holy Sepulchre**
KCIE — **Knight Commander of the Order of the Indian Empire**
KCLJ — **Knight Commander of the Order of St Lazarus of Jerusalem**
KCMG — **Knight Commander of the Order of St Michael and St George**
kcs *or* **kc/s** — **kilocycles per second**
KCSA — **Knight Commander of the Military Order of the Collar of St Agatha of Paterna**
KCSG — **Knight Commander of the Order of St Gregory the Great**
KCSI — **Knight Commander of the Order of the Star of India**
KCSJ — **Knight Commander of the Order of St John of Jerusalem**
KCSS — **Knight Commander of the Order of St Silvester**
KCVO — **Knight Commander of the Royal Victorian Order**
KEAS — *(Aeronautics)* **knots equivalent air-speed**
Ken. — **Kentucky**, a US state
KF — **Det Konservative Folkeparti**, Conservative People's Party, a Danish moderate centre-right political party
kg — symbol for **kilogram**, a unit of mass
KG — **Knight of the Order of the Garter**
KGB — **Komitet Gosudarstvennoy Bezopasnosti** (Russian), Committee of State Security, the Soviet secret police, in control of frontier and general security and the forced-labour system
KGCB — **Knight Grand Cross of the Bath**
Kgs — *(Bible)* **Kings**
KH — **Knight of the Hanoverian Order**
KHS — **Knight of the Order of the Holy Sepulchre**
kHz — **kilohertz**
KIA — *(Military)* **killed in action**
k.i.a.s. *or* **KIAS** — *(Aeronautics)* **knots indicated air-speed**
kJ — **kilojoule**
KJV — **King James Version**, of the Bible
KKK — *(US)* **Ku Klux Klan**
KLH — **Knight of the Legion of Honour**
KLJ — **Knight of the Order of St Lazarus of Jerusalem**

KLM	**Koninklijke Luchtvaart Maatschappij**, Royal Dutch Airlines
km	**kilometre**
KM	**Knight of Malta**
km/h	**kilometres per hour**
KMT	**Kuomintang**, Chinese Nationalist Party, also known as Guomindang
kn	**knot**
Knt	**Knight**
KO	*(Boxing)* **knock out** *or* **knockout**
K of C	**Knights of Columbus**
KP	*(Military)* **kitchen police**, soldiers detailed to assist in kitchen duties
KP	**Knight of the Order of St Patrick**
kph	**kilometres per hour**
Kr	chemical symbol for **krypton**
KrF	**Kristelig Folkeparti**, Christian People's Party, a Danish interdenominational political party
KRL	*(Computing)* **knowledge representation language**
KS	postcode for **Kansas**, a US state
KS	*(Medicine)* **Kaposi's sarcoma**
KSC	**Knight of St Columba**
KSG	**Knight of the Order of St Gregory the Great**
KSJ	**Knight of the Order of St John of Jerusalem**
KSS	**Knight of the Order of St Silvester**
KStJ	**Knight of the Order of St John of Jerusalem**
kt	**karat**
kt	**knot**
Kt.	*(Chess) (US)* **knight**
KT	postcode for **Kingston-upon-Thames**
KT	**Knight of the Order of the Thistle**
KT	**Knight Templar**
Kt Bach.	**Knight Bachelor**
kV	**kilovolt**
kW	**kilowatt**
KW	postcode for **Kirkwall**, Orkney
kWh	**kilowatt hour**
KWIC	**key word in context** (index)
KWOC	**key word out of context** (index)
KWT	**Kuwait**, international vehicle registration

Ky *or* **KY**	postcode for **Kentucky**, a US state
KY	postcode for **Kirkcaldy**
KZ	*(Military)* **killing zone**

L

l	**length**
l	symbol for **litre**
L	**large**; used on clothing labels
L	**learner**; used on the cars of people learning to drive
L	postcode for **Liverpool**
L	**Luxembourg**, international vehicle registration
L	Roman numeral for **50**
La	postcode for **Lancaster**
La	chemical symbol for **lanthanum**
LA	postcode for **Lancaster**
LA	*(US)* **Law Agent**
LA	**Los Angeles**, a US city
LA	postcode for **Louisiana**, a US state
LAA	**light anti-aircraft**
lab.	**laboratory**
Lab.	**Labour**, a member or supporter of the British Labour party
ladar	**laser detection and ranging**
LAES	**Latin American Economic System**, an organization for cooperation in Latin America
LAIA	**Latin American Integration Association**, an organization aiming to create a common market in Latin America
Lam.	*(Bible)* **Lamentations**
LAMDA	**London Academy of Music and Dramatic Art**
LAN	*(Computing)* **local area network**, a network restricted to a single room or building
Lancs	**Lancashire**, an English county
L & NWR	**London and North-Western Railway**
L & SWR	**London and South-Western Railway**
L & YR	**Lancashire and Yorkshire Railway**
Lantirn	*(Military)* **low-altitude navigation and targeting infrared system**
LAO	**Laos**, international vehicle registration

LAR	**Libya**, international vehicle registration
LARSP	**Language Assessment, Remediation, and Screening Procedure**
laser	**light amplification by stimulated emission of radiation**
lat.	**latitude**
Lautro *or* **LAUTRO**	**Life Assurance and Unit Trust Regulatory Organization**
LAV	**light armoured vehicle**
LAV	**Líneas Aéreas Venezolanas**, Venezuelan Airlines
lb	symbol for **pound** (weight)
l.b.	*(Cricket)* **leg bye**
LB	**Liberia**, international vehicle registration
LB & SCR	**London, Brighton, and South Coast Railway**
LBC	**London Broadcasting Company**
LBJ	**Lyndon Baines Johnson**, US president 1963–69
LBO	**leveraged buyout**, the purchase of a controlling proportion of the shares of a company by its own management
LBS	**London Business School**
LBV	**Late Bottled Vintage** (port wine)
lbw	*(Cricket)* **leg before wicket**
lc	*(Printing)* **lower case** (letters)
l.c.	**letter of credit**
LC	**Legislative Council**
LC	**letter of credit**
LC	*(US)* **Library of Congress**
LC	**Lord Chamberlain**
LC	**Lord Chancellor**
L/C	**letter of credit**
LCC	*(Accounting, Computing)* **life-cycle cost** *or* **life-cycle costing**
LCC	**London Chamber of Commerce**
LCD	**liquid-crystal diode**
LCD	**liquid crystal display**
LCDR	**Lieutenant Commander**
LCJ	**Lord Chief Justice**
LCM	**London College of Music**
L-Col	**Lieutenant-Colonel**
L-Corp.	**Lance-Corporal**

LCP **liquid-crystal polymer**
LCP **London College of Printing**
LCpl *or* **L/Cpl** **Lance-Corporal**
LCT **landing craft tank**
Ld **Lord**
LD **lethal dose**
LD postcode for **Llandridnod Wells**
LDC **less-developed country**, a country late in developing an industrial base, and dependent on cash crops and unprocessed minerals
LDDC **London Docklands Development Corporation**
LDL **low-density lipoprotein**
LDN **less-developed nation**, a country late in developing an industrial base, and dependent on cash crops and unprocessed minerals
LDPE **low-density polyethylene**
LDR **light-dependent resistor**, a component of electric circuits used in light-measuring or light-sensing instruments
LDV **Local Defence Volunteers**
LE postcode for **Leicester**
LEA **Local Education Authority**
LEB **London Electricity Board**
LEC **Local Enterprise Company**
LED **light-emitting diode**, a means of displaying symbols in electronic instruments and devices
Leics **Leicestershire**, an English county
LEM **lunar excursion module**
LEP **Large Electron-Positron Collider**, a particle accelerator at the CERN Laboratories near Geneva, Switzerland
LEPRA **Leprosy Relief Association**
Lev. *or* **Levit.** *(Bible)* **Leviticus**
LF **line feed**; used on printers
LF *(Physics)* **low frequency**
LGTB **Local Government Training Board**
LGU **Ladies' Golf Union**
l.h. *or* **LH** **left hand** *or* **left-handed**
LH **luteinizing hormone**, a hormone produced by the pituitary gland
LHA **Lord High Admiral**

LHC **Lord High Chancellor**
l.h.d. **left-hand drive**
LH-RH *(Medicine)* **luteinizing-hormone-releasing hormone**
LHT **Lord High Treasurer**
Li chemical symbol for **lithium**
LI **Light Infantry**
LI *or* **L.I.** **Long Island**, New York
Lib. **Liberal**, member or supporter of the British Liberal party
LIBA **Lloyd's Insurance Brokers' Association**
Lib Dem **Liberal Democrat**, a member of the British Social and Liberal Democratic party
LIBID **London Interbank Bid Rate**
LIBOR **London Interbank Offered Rates**, the main bench mark for much of the Eurodollar loan market
Lic. **Licentiate**
LIC *(Electronics)* **linear integrated circuit**
lidar **light detection and ranging**
Lieut **Lieutenant**
Lieut-Col **Lieutenant-Colonel**
Lieut-Com **Lieutenant-Commander**
Lieut-Gen **Lieutenant-General**
Lieut-Gov **Lieutenant-Governor**
LIFFE **London International Financial Futures Exchange**, one of the exchanges in London where futures contracts are traded
LIFO *(Accounting, Computing)* **last in, first out**
LILO *(Accounting, Computing)* **last in, last out**
LIMEAN **London Inter-Bank Mean Rate**
linac *(Physics)* **linear accelerator**
Lincs **Lincolnshire**, an English county
LIP **life insurance policy**
LIPM **Lister Institute of Preventive Medicine**
LIPS *(Computing)* **logical inferences per second**
LISP *(Computing)* **list processing**, a programming language used in artificial intelligence
LJ **Lord Justice**
Lk. *(Bible)* **Luke**
LL postcode for **Llandudno**
LLNW **low-level nuclear waste**
LLRW **low-level radioactive waste**

LLW **low-level waste**
lm symbol for **lumen**, a unit of luminous flux
LM **Lord Mayor**
LM **lunar module**
LMC **Local Medical Committee**
LME **London Metal Exchange**
LMP **last menstrual period**; used on medical notes
LMR **liquid-metal reactor**
LMR **London Midland Region** (Railways)
LMS **local management of schools**
LMS **London Mathematical Society**
LMS(R) **London, Midland, and Scottish Railway**
LMT **length, mass, time**
LMT **Local Mean Time**
LMX **London Market Excess of Loss** (at Lloyd's)
Ln **Lane**; used in street names
LN postcode for **Lincoln**
LNER **London and North Eastern Railway**
LNG **liquefied natural gas**
loc. *(Grammar)* **locative**
loc. cit. *loco citato* (Latin), at the place cited; used in reference citations
L of N **League of Nations**, an international organization formed after World War I to solve international disputes by arbitration
LOFT **low-frequency radio telescope**
log **logarithm**
LOI **lunar orbit insertion**
long. **longitude**
Lonrho **London Rhodesian**, an industrial conglomerate
loran **long-range navigation**
Lot **Polskie Linie Lotnicze**, Polish Air Lines
low-cal **low in calories**
lox *or* **LOX** **liquid oxygen**
l.p. **low pressure**
LP **long-playing** (record)
LP **low pressure**
LPG **liquefied petroleum gas**
LPLC **low-pressure liquid chromatography**
lpm **lines per minute**

LPN	*(US)* **Licensed Practical Nurse**
LPO	**London Philharmonic Orchestra**
LPS	**Lord Privy Seal**
LQ	*(Computing)* **letter quality**
Lr	chemical symbol for **lawrencium**
LR	**Lloyd's Register** (of Shipping)
LRC	**London Rowing Club**
LREC	**Local Research Ethics Committee**
LRMTS	Laser Ranging Marker Target System, a system used for guiding missiles accurately to their target
LRT	**London Regional Transport**
LRV	**lunar roving vehicle**
LS	postcode for **Leeds**
LS	**Lesotho**, international vehicle registration
LS	**London Sinfonietta**
LSD	*(Computing)* **least significant digit**
LSD	**lysergic acid diethylamide**, a hallucinogenic drug
LSE	**London School of Economics and Political Science**
L-Sgt	**Lance-Sergeant**
LSHTM	**London School of Hygiene and Tropical Medicine**
LSI	*(Electronics)* **large-scale integration**, the technology that enables whole electrical circuits to be etched into a very small piece of semiconducting material
LSJ	**London School of Journalism**
LSO	**London Symphony Orchestra**
LSS	**life-support system**
LST	**Local Standard Time**
lt	**light**
l.t.	**long ton**
Lt	**Lieutenant**
LT	**Lawn Tennis**
LT	**London Transport**
LT	**long ton**
LTA	**Lawn Tennis Association**
LT & SR	**London, Tilbury, and Southend Railway**
LTB	**London Tourist Board**
Lt-Cdr	**Lieutenant-Commander**
Lt-Cmdr	**Lieutenant-Commander**
Lt-Col	**Lieutenant-Colonel**
Lt-Com	**Lieutenant-Commander**

Ltd	**Limited**
Lt-Gen	**Lieutenant-General**
Lt-Gov	**Lieutenant-Governor**
LTH	*(Medicine)* **luteotrophic hormone**
Lt Inf.	**Light Infantry**
LTJG	**Lieutenant Junior Grade**
LTOM	**London Traded Options Market**
Lu	chemical symbol for **lutetium**
LU	postcode for **Luton**
LUG	*(Computing)* **local users' group**
LV	**licensed victualler**
LV	**luncheon voucher**
LVA	**Licensed Victuallers' Association**
LVLO	**Local Vehicle Licensing Office**
LW	*(Radio)* **long wave**
LWRA	**London Waste Regulation Authority**
LWT	**London Weekend Television**, a television company
lx	symbol for **lux**, a unit of illuminance
l.y.	**light year**
LZ	**landing zone**

M

m	symbol for metre, a unit of length
m.	*(Cricket)* **maiden** (over)
m.	**male**
m.	**married**
m.	**mile**
M	*(Aeronautics)* symbol for **Mach**
M	**Malta**, international vehicle registration
M	postcode for **Manchester**
M	*(Physics)* **mass**
M	**medium**; used on clothing labels
M	***Monsieur*** (French), Mr *or* Sir
M	**Motorway**; used for road numbers, e.g. the M40
M	Roman numeral for **1,000**
M.	**Marquess**
M.	**Marquis**
mA	**milliampere**
Ma	*(Aeronautics)* symbol for **Mach number**
MA	postcode for **Massachusetts**, a US state
MA	**Master of Arts**
MA	*(Psychology)* **mental age**
MA	**Morocco**, international vehicle registration
MAA	**Manufacturers' Agents Association of Great Britain**
MAA	**master-at-arms**
MAAF	**Mediterranean Allied Air Forces**
MAAT	**Member of the Association of Accounting Technicians**
MAC	*(Television)* **multiplexed analogue components**
MACE	**Member of the Association of Conference Executives**
MACM	**Member of the Association of Computing Machines**
MAD	**major affective disorder**
MAD	**mutual assured destruction**, the basis of the theory of deterrence by possession of nuclear weapons
MADO	**Member of the Association of Dispensing Opticians**
MA(Ed)	**Master of Arts in Education**

MAEE **Marine Aircraft Experimental Establishment**
MAFF **Ministry of Agriculture, Fisheries, and Food**, a British government department
mag. **magazine**
maglev **magnetic levitation**, a form of high-speed surface transport using superconductive magnets to propel and support a train above a track
MAIB **Marine Accident Investment Branch**
maj. **major**
Maj **Major**
Maj-Gen **Major General**
Mal. *(Bible)* **Malachi**
MAL **Malaysia**, international vehicle registration
MAMEME **Member of the Association of Mining Electrical and Mechanical Engineers**
Man. **Manitoba**, a Canadian province
M & B **May and Baker**, a pharmaceutical company
M & B **Mills and Boon**, publishers of romantic novels
Man. Dir. **Managing Director**
M & S **Marks & Spencer plc**
MANWEB **Merseyside and North Wales Electricity Board**
MAOT **Member of the Association of Occupational Therapists**
MAP **Ministry of Aircraft Production**
MARC **machine-readable cataloguing**
March. **Marchioness**
Marq. **Marquess**
Marq. **Marquis**
MARV *(Military)* **manoeuvrable re-entry vehicle**
mas. *or* **masc.** **masculine**
MASCAM *(Electronics)* **masking-pattern adaptive sub-band coding and multiplexing**
MASCE **Member of the American Society of Civil Engineers**
maser **microwave amplification by stimulated emission of radiation**, a high-frequency microwave amplifier or oscillator
MASH *(US)* **mobile army surgical hospital**
Mass. **Massachusetts**, a US state
mat. **matinée**
MATS **Military Air Transport Service**

MATSA **Managerial Administrative Technical Staff Association**
Matt. *(Bible)* **Matthew**
MATV **master antenna television**
max. **maximum**
mb *(Computing)* **megabyte**
mb **millibar**
Mb *(Computing)* **megabyte**
MB **Manitoba**, a Canadian province
MB *(Computing)* **megabyte**
MBAcA **Member of the British Acupuncture Association**
mbar **millibar**
MBASW **Member of the British Association of Social Workers**
MBC **metropolitan borough council**
MBC **municipal borough council**
MBCS **Member of the British Computer Society**
MBE **Member of the Order of the British Empire**
MBHI **Member of the British Horological Institute**
MBIFD **Member of the British Institute of Funeral Directors**
MBKSTS **Member of the British Kinematograph, Sound, and Television Society**
MBO **management buyout**
MBOU **Member of the British Ornithologists' Union**
MBPICS **Member of the British Production and Inventory Control Society**
MBPsS **Member of the British Psychological Society**
MBT *(Military)* **main battle tank**
Mbyte *(Computing)* **megabyte**
m.c. **motorcycle**
m/c **machine**
m/c **motorcycle**
MC **Marine Corps**
MC **Master of Ceremonies**
MC **Medical Corps**
MC *(US)* **Member of Congress**
MC **Military Cross**
MC **Monaco**, international vehicle registration
MCA **Management Consultants' Association**
MCA *(Computing)* (trademark) **micro channel architecture**
MCB *(Computing)* **memory control block**
MCB *(Military)* **multiple cratering bomblets**

MCBSI **Member of the Chartered Building Societies Institute**
MCC **Marylebone Cricket Club**
MCC **metropolitan county council**
MCD **Movement for Christian Democracy**
MCGA *(Computing)* **multicolour graphics array**
MChS **Member of the Society of Chiropodists**
MCIBSE **Member of the Chartered Institution of Building Services Engineers**
MCIM **Member of the Chartered Institute of Marketing**
MCIOB **Member of the Chartered Institute of Building**
MCIS **Member of the Institute of Chartered Secretaries and Administrators (formerly Chartered Institute of Secretaries)**
MCIT **Member of the Chartered Institute of Transport**
MCMES **Member of the Civil and Mechanical Engineers' Society**
MConsE **Member of the Association of Consulting Engineers**
MCOphth **Men ber of the College of Ophthalmologists**
MCPO **Master Chief Petty Officer**
MCPP **Member of the College of Pharmacy Practice**
MCPS **Member of the College of Physicians and Surgeons**
MCSP **Member of the Chartered Society of Physiotherapy**
MCST **Member of the College of Speech Therapists**
MCT **Member of the Association of Corporate Treasurers**
Md **Maryland**, a US state
Md chemical symbol for **mendelevium**
MD ***Medicinae Doctor*** (Latin), Doctor of Medicine
MD **managing director**
MD postcode for **Maryland**, a US state
MDA *(Computing)* **monochrome display adaptor**
MDA **Muscular Dystrophy Association**
MDC **metropolitan district council**
MDC **more developed country**
Mdlle ***Mademoiselle*** (French), Miss
Mdm **Madam**
MDMA **methylenedioxymethamphetamine**, a psychedelic drug, also known as ecstasy
Mdme ***Madame*** (French), Mrs
mdnt **midnight**
MDR **minimum daily requirement**

mdse **merchandise**
MDT *(US)* **Mountain Daylight Time**
Me **Maine**, a US state
ME postcode for **Maine**, a US state
ME **Mechanical Engineer**
ME postcode for **Medway**
ME **Middle East**
ME **Middle English**
ME **myalgic encephalomyelitis**, a debilitating condition also known as postviral fatigue syndrome, with symptoms that include muscular pain, weakness, and depression
MEB **Midlands Electricity Board**
MEC **Member of the Executive Council**
MECI **Member of the Institute of Employment Consultants**
MECO **main engine cut off**
med. **medium**
Med. **Mediterranean**
MEd **Master of Education**
meg *(Computing)* **megabyte**
memo **memorandum**
Mencap *or* **MENCAP** **Royal Society for Mentally Handicapped Children and Adults**
MEO **Marine Engineering Officer**
m.e.p. *or* **MEP** *(Physics)* **mean effective pressure**
MEP **Member of the European Parliament**
MERLIN *(Astronomy)* **Multi-Element Radio-linked Interferometer Network**
Messrs *Messieur*s (French), Gentlemen *or* Sirs
met. **meteorological**
Met **Metropolitan Opera House**, in New York
Met **Metropolitan Police**
MetE **Metallurgical Engineer**
Meth. **Methodist**
MeV **mega-electronvolt**
MEX **Mexico**, international vehicle registration
MEXE **Military Engineering Experimental Establishment**
mf *(Music)* ***mezzo forte*** (Italian), moderately loudly
mF *(Physics)* **millifarad**

MF **medium frequency**
m/f *or* **M/F** **male** *or* **female**; used in advertisements
MFARCS **Member of the Faculty of Anaesthetists of the Royal College of Surgeons**
MFCM **Member of the Faculty of Community Medicine**
MFH **Master of Foxhounds**
MFHom **Member of the Faculty of Homeopathy**
MFLOPS *(Computing)* **million floating-point operations per second**
MFM *(Computing)* **modified frequency modulation**
MFN **most favoured nation**
MFOM **Member of the Faculty of Occupational Medicine**
MFPA **Mouth and Foot Painting Artists**
m. ft. ***mistura fiat*** (Latin), let a mixture be made; used in prescriptions
MFV **motor fleet vessel**
mg symbol for **milligram**
Mg chemical symbol for **magnesium**
MG **Major General**
MG **Morris Garages**, manufacturer of the MG sports car
MGC **Machine Gun Corps**
MGI **Member of the Institute of Certified Grocers**
M. Glam **Mid Glamorgan**, a Welsh county
MGM **Metro-Goldwyn-Mayer**, a US film production company
MGN **Mirror Group Newspapers**
Mgr **Manager**
Mgr ***Monseigneur*** (French), my lord
Mgr ***Monsignor*** (Italian), my lord
mH *(Physics)* **millihenry**
MH **Medal of Honor**, the highest award given by the US army and navy for gallantry in action
MHA **Methodist Homes for the Aged**
MHCIMA **Member of the Hotel Catering and Institutional Management Association**
MHD **magnetohydrodynamics**, science concerned with the behaviour of ionized gases or liquid in a magnetic field
MHR *(US, Australia)* **Member of the House of Representatives**
MHRA **Modern Humanities Research Association**
MHRF **Mental Health Research Fund**
MHS *(Computing)* **message-handling system**

MHz **megahertz**
mi symbol for **mile**
MI postcode for **Michigan**, a US state
MI **military intelligence**
MI *(Medicine)* **myocardial infarction**
MIA *(Military)* **missing in action**
MIAA&S **Member of the Incorporated Association of Architects and Surveyors**
MIAeE **Member of the Institute of Aeronautical Engineers**
MIAgrE **Member of the Institution of Agricultural Engineers**
MIAM **Member of the Institute of Administrative Management**
MIBF **Member of the Institute of British Foundrymen**
MIBiol **Member of the Institute of Biology**
MIBritE **Member of the Institution of British Engineers**
Mic. *(Bible)* **Micah**
MICE **Member of the Institution of Civil Engineers**
MICFor **Member of the Institute of Chartered Foresters**
Mich. **Michigan**, a US state
MIChemE **Member of the Institution of Chemical Engineers**
MICorrST **Member of the Institution of Corrosion Science and Technology**
MICR *(Computing)* **magnetic-ink character recognition**
MICS **Member of the Institute of Chartered Shipbrokers**
MICV **mechanized infantry combat vehicle**
MIDAS **missile defence alarm system**
Middx **Middlesex**, a former English county
Midi *or* **MIDI** *(Computing)* **musical instrument digital interface**, an interface enabling electronic instruments to be connected to a computer
MIDPM **Member of the Institute of Data Processing Management**
MIED **Member of the Institution of Engineering Designers**
MIEE **Member of the Institution of Electrical Engineers**
MIEI **Member of the Institution of Engineering Inspection**
MIEx **Member of the Institute of Export**
MIExpE **Member of the Institute of Explosives Engineers**
MIFA **Member of the Institute of Field Archaeologists**
MIFF **Member of the Institute of Freight Forwarders**
MIFirE **Member of the Institute of Fire Engineers**

MiG a Soviet jet fighter, named after its designers **Mikoyan and Gurevich**
MIGasE **Member of the Institution of Gas Engineers**
MIGeol **Member of the Institution of Geologists**
MIH **Member of the Institute of Housing**
MIHort **Member of the Institute of Horticulture**
MIHT **Member of the Institution of Highways and Transportation**
MIIM **Member of the Institute of Industrial Managers**
MIInfSc **Member of the Institute of Information Sciences**
MIL **Member of the Institute of Linguists**
MILGA **Member of the Institute of Local Government Administrators**
MILocoE **Member of the Institution of Locomotive Engineers**
MIM **Member of the Institute of Metals**
MIMarE **Member of the Institute of Marine Engineers**
MIMC **Member of the Institute of Management Consultants**
MIMechE **Member of the Institution of Mechanical Engineers**
MIMGTechE **Member of the Institution of Mechanical and General Technician Engineers**
MIMI **Member of the Institute of the Motor Industry**
MIMinE **Member of the Institution of Mining Engineers**
MIMM **Member of the Institution of Mining and Metallurgy**
min. **minimum**
min. **minute**
Minn. **Minnesota**, a US state
MINucE **Member of the Institution of Nuclear Engineers**
MIOSH **Member of the Institution of Occupational Safety and Health**
m.i.p. **mean indicated pressure**
MIP **maximum investment plan**
MIP **Member of the Institute of Plumbing**
MIPA **Member of the Institute of Practitioners in Advertising**
MIPM **Member of the Institute of Personnel Management**
MIPR **Member of the Institute of Public Relations**
MIProdE **Member of the Institute of Production Engineers**
mips *or*
MIPS *(Computing)* **million instructions per second**
MIQ **Member of the Institute of Quarrying**
MIRAS **mortgage interest relief at source**

MIRT **Member of the Institute of Reprographic Technicians**
MIRTE **Member of the Institute of Road Transport Engineers**
MIRV **multiple independently targeted re-entry vehicle**, the nuclear-warhead-carrying part of a ballistic missile that splits off in midair from the main body. They can attack separate targets over a wide area.
MIS **Member of the Institute of Statisticians**
misc. **miscellaneous**
MISD *(Computing)* **multiple instruction (stream), single data (stream)**
MIStructE **Member of the Institution of Structural Engineers**
MITA **Member of the Industrial Transport Association**
MITD **Member of the Institute of Training and Development**
MITE **Member of the Institution of Electrical and Electronics Technician Engineers**
MITT **Member of the Institute of Travel and Tourism**
Mitts **minutes of telecommunications traffic**
MIWEM **Member of the Institution of Water and Environmental Management**
MJ **megajoule**
MJI **Member of the Institute of Journalists**
MJS **Member of the Japan Society**
Mk **mark**
Mk. *(Bible)* **Mark**
MK postcode for **Milton Keynes**
mks *or* **MKS** **metre kilogram second**
mkt **market**
ml *or* **mL** symbol for **millilitre**
ML postcode for **Motherwell**
MLA **Member of the Legislative Assembly**
MLC **Meat and Livestock Commission**
MLF **multilateral (nuclear) force**
Mlle *Mademoiselle* (French), Miss
MLO **Military Liaison Officer**
MLR **minimum lending rate**, the rate of interest at which the Bank of England lends to the money market
MLSO **Medical Laboratory Scientific Officer**
mm symbol for **millimetre**
MM *Messieurs* (French), Gentlemen *or* Sirs
MM **Military Medal**

MA **Metropolitan Museum of Art**, in New York

MMB **Milk Marketing Board**

MMC **Monopolies and Mergers Commission**, a British government body which investigates the risk of a monopoly being created by a company merger or takeover

MMDS *(Radio)* **multipoint microwave distribution system**

Mme ***Madame*** (French), Mrs

mmf *(Physics)* **magnetomotive force**

mmHg symbol for **millimetre of mercury**, a unit of pressure

MMR **measles, mumps, rubella** (vaccine)

MMS **Marine Meteorological Services**

MMS **Member of the Institute of Management Services**

MMU *(Computing)* **memory management unit**

Mn chemical symbol for **manganese**

MN **Merchant Navy**

MN postcode for **Minnesota**, a US state

MNAD **Multinational Airmobile Division**, part of NATO

MNC **multinational company**

MNE **multinational enterprise**

MNI **Member of the Nautical Institute**

mo. **month**

m.o. **mail order**

m.o. ***modus operandi*** (Latin), method of operating

Mo chemical symbol for **molybdenum**

MO **Medical Officer**

MO postcode for **Missouri**, a US state

MO ***modus operandi*** (Latin), method of operating

MO **money order**

MOBS **multiple-orbit bombardment system**, a nuclear weapon system

MoC **mother of the chapel**, a trade union office

mod. **moderate**

mod. **modern**

MoD *or* **MOD** **Ministry of Defence**, a British government department

modem *(Computing)* **modulator/demodulator**, a device for transmitting computer data over telephone lines

MOEH **Medical Officer for Environmental Health**

MOH **Medical Officer of Health**

MOI **Ministry of Information**

mol symbol for **mole**, a unit of amount of substance

MOL manned orbital laboratory
mol. wt. molecular weight
m.o.m. middle of month
MOMI **Museum of the Moving Image**, in London
Mont. **Montana**, a US state
MOR **middle-of-the-road**
MORI **Market and Opinion Research Institute**
mor. sol. ***more solito*** (Latin), in the usual manner; used in prescriptions
MoT *or* MOT **Ministry of Transport**
MOVE **Men Over Violence**, an association for men who are violent to their wives
MOW **Movement for the Ordination of Women**
MOX **mixed oxide**
mp *or* m.p. **melting point**
MP **Member of Parliament**
MP **Metropolitan Police**
MP *(US)* **Military Police** *or* **Military Policeman**
MP **Mounted Police** *or* **Mounted Policeman**
MPA **Master Printers Association**
MPA **Member of the Parliamentary Assembly of Northern Ireland**
MPBW **Ministry of Public Building and Works**
MPEA **Member of the Physical Education Association**
mpg **miles per gallon**
MPG **main professional grade**, the basic salary for a teacher in Britain
mph **miles per hour**
MPLA **Movimento Popular de Libertação de Angola** (Portuguese), Popular Movement for the Liberation of Angola, a socialist organization founded in the 1950s that sought to free Angola from Portuguese rule
MPO **Metropolitan Police Office**
MPS **Medical Protection Society**
MPS **Member of the Philological Society**
MPS **Member of the Physical Society**
Mr **Mister**
MR **magnetic resonance**
MRA **Moral Rearmament**, an international movement calling for 'moral and spiritual renewal'

MRAC	**Member of the Royal Agricultural College**
MRAeS	**Member of the Royal Aeronautical Society**
MRAS	**Member of the Royal Asiatic Society**
MRBM	**medium-range ballistic missile**
MRBS	**Member of the Royal Botanic Society**
MRC	**Medical Research Council**
MRCA	**multirole combat aircraft**
MRCGP	**Member of the Royal College of General Practitioners**
MRC-LMB	**Medical Research Council Laboratory for Molecular Biology**
MRCO	**Member of the Royal College of Organists**
MRCOG	**Member of the Royal College of Obstetricians and Gynaecologists**
MRCP	**Member of the Royal College of Physicians**
MRCPath	**Member of the Royal College of Pathologists**
MRCPE	**Member of the Royal College of Physicians of Edinburgh**
MRCPGlas	**Member of the Royal College of Physicians and Surgeons of Glasgow**
MRCPI	**Member of the Royal College of Physicians of Ireland**
MRCPsych	**Member of the Royal College of Psychiatrists**
MRCS	**Member of the Royal College of Surgeons**
MRCSE	**Member of the Royal College of Surgeons of Edinburgh**
MRCSI	**Member of the Royal College of Surgeons of Ireland**
MRCVS	**Member of the Royal College of Veterinary Surgeons**
MRE	*(Military)* **meal ready-to-eat**
MRE	**Microbiological Research Establishment**
MRG	**Minority Rights Group**
MRGS	**Member of the Royal Geographical Society**
MRH	**Member of the Royal Household**
MRHS	**Member of the Royal Horticultural Society**
MRI	**magnetic resonance imaging**, a diagnostic scanning system that yields finely detailed three-dimensional images of body structures without exposing the patient to radiation
MRI	**Member of the Royal Institution**
MRIA	**Member of the Royal Irish Academy**
MRIAI	**Member of the Royal Institute of the Architects of Ireland**
MRIN	**Member of the Royal Institute of Navigation**

MRINA	**Member of the Royal Institution of Naval Architects**
MRIPHH	**Member of the Royal Institute of Public Health and Hygiene**
MRM	**mechanically recovered meat**
MRMetS	**Member of the Royal Meteorological Society**
mRNA	**messenger RNA**
MRO	**Member of the Register of Osteopaths**
MRP	**manufacturer's recommended price**
MRPharmS	**Member of the Royal Pharmaceutical Society**
Mrs	**Mistress**, title given to a married woman
MRS	**Magnetic resonance spectroscopy**
MRSC	**Member of the Royal Society of Chemistry**
MRSH	**Member of the Royal Society for the Promotion of Health**
MRSL	**Member of the Royal Society of Literature**
MRSM	**Member of the Royal Society of Medicine**
MRSM	**Member of the Royal Society of Musicians of Great Britain**
MRSPE	**Member of the Royal Society of Painter-Etchers and Engravers**
MRSPP	**Member of the Royal Society of Portrait Painters**
MRST	**Member of the Royal Society of Teachers**
MRTPI	**Member of the Royal Town Planning Institute**
MRUSI	**Member of the Royal United Service Institution**
MRV	*(Military)* **multiple re-entry vehicle**
MRVA	**Member of the Rating and Valuation Association**
ms	**manuscript**
ms	**millisecond**
m/s	**metre per second**
Ms	Miss *or* **Mrs**; used by married or unmarried women
MS	**Mauritius**, international vehicle registration
MS	***memoriae sacrum*** (Latin), sacred to the memory of
MS	**milestone**; used on maps
MS	**Mississippi**, a US state
MS	**multiple sclerosis**, an incurable chronic disease of the central nervous system
MSA	**Member of the Society of Apothecaries**
MSA	**Mineralogical Society of America**
MS & R	**Merchant Shipbuilding and Repairs**
MSAutE	**Member of the Society of Automobile Engineers**

MSc **Master of Science**
MSC **Manchester Ship Canal**
MSC **Manpower Services Commission**, former name of the Training Agency
MSCI Index **Morgan Stanley Capital International World Index**
MS-DOS *(Computing)* (trademark) **MicroSoft Disk Operating System**
MSE **Member of the Society of Engineers**
MSF **Manufacturing, Science, and Finance**, a UK trade union
MSF **Médecins sans frontières** (French), Doctors Without Frontiers, a charitable body
MSG **monosodium glutamate**, a powder which is used to enhance the flavour of some foods
Msgr ***Monseigneur*** (French), my lord
Msgr ***Monsignor*** (Italian), my lord
MSH **Master of Staghounds**
MSI *(Electronics)* **medium-scale integration**
MSIAD **Member of the Society of Industrial Artists and Designers**
msl *or* **MSL** **mean sea level**
MSM **Meritorious Service Medal**
MSO **Member of the Society of Osteopaths**
MSQ **managing service quality**
MSR **Member of the Society of Radiographers**
MSR *(Military)* **missile-site radar**
MSS **Member of the Royal Statistical Society**
MST *(US)* **Mountain Standard Time**
MSTD **Member of the Society of Typographic Designers**
m.t. **metric ton**
Mt **Mount** *or* **Mountain**
Mt. *(Bible)* **Matthew**
MT postcode for **Montana**, a US state
MT *(US)* **Mountain Time**
MTA **Music Trades' Association**
MTAI **Member of the Institute of Travel Agents**
MTB **motor torpedo boat**
MTBE **methyl t-butyl ether**, a substance added to petrol to prevent knocking
MTC **Mechanized Transport Corps**
MTCA **Ministry of Transport and Civil Aviation**

MTO **made to order**
Mt Rev **Most Reverend**
MU **Musicians' Union**, a British trade union
MUF *(Telecommunications)* **maximum usable frequency**
MUFTI *(Military)* **minimum use of force tactical intervention**
mV **millivolt**
MV **megavolt**
MVD **Ministertvo Vnutrennykh Del** (Russian), Ministry of Internal Affairs, 1946–60
MVEE **Military Vehicles and Engineering Establishment**
MVL **motor-vehicle licence**
MVO **Member of the Royal Victorian Order**
MVP *(Baseball)* **most valuable player**
mW **milliwatt**
MW **Malawi**, international vehicle registration
MW **Master of Wine**
MW *(Radio)* **medium wave**
MW **megawatt**
MW **Most Worshipful**
MW **Most Worthy**
MWeldI **Member of the Welding Institute**
Mx **Middlesex**, a former English county
MX **missile experimental**, a land-based intercontinental nuclear missile, known as the Peacekeeper

N

n.	**noun**
N	*(Chess)* **knight**
N	**Nationalist**
N	symbol for **newton**, a unit of force
N	chemical symbol for **nitrogen**
N	**north**
N	postcode for **north London**
N	**Norway**, international vehicle registration
n/a	**not applicable**
Na	chemical symbol for **sodium**
NA	**Netherlands Antilles**, international vehicle registration
NA	**North America**
NAACP	**National Association for the Advancement of Colored People**, a US civil rights organization dedicated to ending inequality for African-Americans by nonviolent protest
Naafi *or* **NAAFI**	**Navy Army and Air Force Institutes**, an association providing canteens for HM British Forces
NAAS	**National Agricultural Advisory Service**
NAB	**National Advisory Body for Public Sector Higher Education**
NABC	**National Association of Boys' Clubs**
NABS	**National Advertising Benevolent Society**
NAC	**National Advisory Council**
NAC	**National Agriculture Centre**
NAC	**National Association for the Childless**
NACAB	**National Association of Citizens Advice Bureaux**
NACCB	**National Accreditation Council for Certification Bodies**
NACNE	**National Advisory Committee on Nutrition Education**
NACOSS	**National Approved Council for Security Systems**
NACRO	**National Association for the Care and Resettlement of Offenders**
NAD	**no abnormality detected**; used on medical notes

NADEC	**National Association of Development Education Centres**
NADFAS	**National Association of Decorative and Fine Arts Societies**
NADGE	**NATO Air Defence Ground Environment**
NAEA	**National Association of Estate Agents**
NAEW	**NATO Airborne Early Warning**
NAFMCS	**National Association of Family Mediation and Conciliation Services**
NAFTA	**New Zealand and Australia Free Trade Agreement**
NAGC	**National Association for Gifted Children**
Nah.	*(Bible)* **Nahum**
NAHAT	**National Association of Health Authorities and Trusts**
NAHT	**National Association of Head Teachers**
NAI	**nonaccidental injury**
NAIRU	*(Economics)* **nonaccelerating inflation rate of unemployment**
NAITA	**National Association of Independent Travel Agents**
NALGO	**National and Local Government Officers' Association**
N. Am.	**North America**
NAMAS	**National Measurement and Accreditation Service**
NAMCW	**National Association of Maternal and Child Welfare**
NAMMA	**NATO MRCA Management Agency**
NAMS	*(US)* **national air-monitoring sites**
N & P	**National and Provincial Building Society**
NAO	**National Audit Office**
napalm	**naphthenic and palmitic acids**, a fuel used in flamethrowers and incendiary bombs
NAPF	**National Association of Pension Funds**
NAPO	**National Association of Probation Officers**, a trade union
NAPT	**National Association for the Prevention of Tuberculosis**
NAS	*(US)* **National Academy of Sciences**
NAS	**naval air station**
NAS	**Noise Abatement Society**
Nasa *or* NASA	**National Aeronautics and Space Administration**, a US agency for spaceflight and aeronautical research
NASUWT	**National Association of Schoolmasters, Union of Women Teachers**, a British trade union

NATFHE **National Association of Teachers in Further and Higher Education**, a British trade union

NATLAS **National Testing Laboratory Accreditation Scheme**

Nato *or* **NATO** **North Atlantic Treaty Organization**, an organization set up in 1949 to provide for the collective defence of Western Europe and the US against the USSR

NATS **National Air Traffic Services**

NATSOPA **National Society of Operative Printers, Graphical, and Media Personnel**

Nav.E. **Naval Engineer**

NAVSAT **navigational satellite**

NAWC **National Association of Women's Clubs**

NAWO **National Alliance of Women's Organizations**

NAYT **National Association of Youth Theatres**

Nazi ***Nationalsozialisten*** (German), National Socialist

nb *(Cricket)* **no ball**

nb *or* **n.b.** ***nota bene*** (Latin), note well

Nb chemical symbol for **niobium**

NB **New Brunswick**, a Canadian province

NB ***nota bene*** (Latin), note well

NBA **Net Book Agreement**

NBC **National Broadcasting Company**, a US television and radio network

NBC **nuclear, biological, and chemical** (weapons or warfare)

NBI **National Benevolent Institution**

NBL **National Book League**

N-bomb **neutron bomb**

NBPI **National Board for Prices and Incomes**

NBRI **National Building Research Institute**

NBS **National Bureau of Standards**, the US federal standards organization, on whose technical standards all US weights and measures are based

NC postcode for **North Carolina**, a US state

NC **numerical control** *or* **numerically controlled**

NCA **National Childminding Association**

NCA **National Cricket Association**

NCB **National Children's Bureau**

NCB **no claim bonus**

NCBW **nuclear, chemical, and biological warfare**

NCC **National Computing Centre**
NCC **National Consumer Council**
NCC **National Curriculum Council**
NCC **Nature Conservancy Council**
NCCI **National Committee for Commonwealth Immigrants**
NCCJ **National Conference of Christians and Jews**
NCDAD **National Council for Diplomas in Art and Design**
NCDL **National Canine Defence League**
NCET **National Council for Educational Technology**
NCLC **National Council of Labour Colleges**
NCO **noncommissioned officer**
NCP **National Car Parks Ltd**
NCPS **noncontributory pension scheme**
NCR **National Cash Register Company Ltd**
NCRL **National Chemical Research Laboratory**
NCSE **National Council for Special Education**
NCT **National Chamber of Trade**
NCT **National Childbirth Trust**
NCU **National Communications Union, a British trade union**
NCU **National Cyclists' Union**
NCVCCO **National Council of Voluntary Child Care Organizations**
NCVO **National Council for Voluntary Organizations**
NCVQ **National Council for Vocational Qualifications**
NCW **National Council of Women** (of Great Britain)
n.d. **no date** *or* **not dated**
Nd chemical symbol for **neodymium**
ND **New Democracy Party**, a Greek centre-right political party
ND **postcode for North Dakota**, a US state
N. Dak. **North Dakota**, a US state
NDB *(Aeronautics)* **nondirectional beacon**
NDC **National Defence College**
NDC **National Dairy Council**
NDCS **National Deaf Children's Society**
NDE **near-death experience**
NDIC **National Defence Industries Council**
NDP **New Democratic Party**, a Canadian moderate left-of-centre political party
NDPS **National Data Processing Service**
NDSF **National Diploma of the Society of Floristry**

Ne	chemical symbol for **neon**
NE	**Naval Engineer**
NE	postcode for Nebraska, a US state
NE	postcode for **Newcastle**
NE	**New England**, an area in the NE United States
NE	**northeast**
NE	**nuclear energy**
NEB	**National Enterprise Board**
NEB	**New English Bible**
Nebr.	**Nebraska**, a US state
NEBSS	**National Examinations Board for Supervisory Studies**
NEC	**National Executive Committee**
NEC	**National Exhibition Centre**, in Birmingham, England
NEC	**Nippon Electric Company** (Japan)
NECCTA	**National Educational Closed Circuit Television Association**
NECInst	**North East Coast Institution of Engineers and Shipbuilders**
NEDC	**National Economic Development Council**, the British forum for economic consultation between government, management, and trade unions
NEDO	**National Economic Development Office**
NEEB	**North Eastern Electricity Board**
neg.	**negative**
Neh.	*(Bible)* **Nehemiah**
NEH	**National Endowment for the Humanities**
NEL	**National Engineering Laboratory**
NERC	**Natural Environment Research Council**, a British organization established to undertake and support research in the earth sciences, advise on protecting the environment, and support education and training of scientists
NET	*(US)* **National Educational Television**
n. et m.	***nocte et mane*** (Latin), night and morning; used in prescriptions
Nev.	**Nevada**, a US state
Newf	**Newfoundland**, a Canadian province
New M.	**New Mexico**, a US state
NF	**National Front**, a British extreme right-wing political party
NF	**Newfoundland**, a Canadian province
NFBTE	**National Federation of Building Trades Employers**

NFC *(US)* **National Football Conference**
NFC **National Freight Consortium**
Nfd. **Newfoundland**, a Canadian province
NFER **National Foundation for Educational Research**
NFFPT **National Federation of Fruit and Potato Trades**
NFHA **National Federation of Housing Associations**
NFL *(Canada and US)* **National Football League**
Nfld. **Newfoundland**, a Canadian province
NFMS **National Federation of Music Societies**
NFS **National Fire Service**
NFS *(Computing)* **network file service** or **network file system**
NFS **not for sale**
NFSE **National Federation of Self-Employed** (and Small Businesses)
NFT **National Film Theatre**
NFU **National Farmers' Union**
NFWI **National Federation of Women's Institutes**
NG **National Guard**, a US militia recruited by each state
NG postcode for **Nottingham**
NGNP **nominal gross national product**
NGO **nongovernmental organization**
NGS **nuclear generating station**
NGTE **National Gas Turbine Establishment**
NGV **natural-gas vehicle**
NH postcode for New Hampshire, a US state
NHBC **National House-Building Council**
NHBRC **National House-Builders' Registration Certificate**
NHI **National Health Insurance**
NHR **National Housewives Register**
NHS **National Health Service**, the provision of medical care by the British government
NHTPC **National Housing and Town Planning Council**
Ni chemical symbol for **nickel**
NI **National Insurance**
NI **Northern Ireland**
NI **North Island**, New Zealand
NIAB **National Institute of Agricultural Botany**
NIACRO **Northern Ireland Association for the Care and Resettlement of Offenders**
NIAE **National Institute of Agricultural Engineering**

NIAID **National Institute of Allergy and Infectious Diseases**

NIBSC **National Institute for Biological Standards Control**

NIC **newly industrialized country**, a country that has recently experienced a breakthrough into manufacturing and rapid export-led growth. Examples are Taiwan, Hong Kong, Singapore and South Korea.

NIC **National Incomes Commission**

NIC **Nicaragua**, international vehicle registration

NICAM *(Electronics)* **near-instantaneous commanded audio multiplex**

NICEC **National Institute for Careers Education and Counselling**

NICG **Nationalized Industries Chairmen's Group**

NICRA **Northern Ireland Civil Rights Association**

NICS **Northern Ireland Civil Service**

NICU **neonatal intensive care unit**

NID **National Institute for the Deaf**

NID **National Institute of Design**

NIEO **New International Economic Order**

NIES **Northern Ireland Electricity Service**

NIESR **National Institute of Economic and Social Research**

NIHCA **Northern Ireland Hotels and Caterers Association**

NIHE **National Institute for Higher Education**, in Ireland

NII **Nuclear Installations Inspectorate**

NILP **Northern Ireland Labour Party**

Nimby *or* **NIMBY** **not in my back yard**, describing an attitude of resistance to building developments, power stations, etc.

NIMH **National Institute of Medical Herbalists**

NIMR **National Institute for Medical Research**

NIRC **National Industrial Relations Court**

NIREX **Nuclear Industry Radioactive Waste Executive**

NISTRO **Northern Ireland Science and Technology Regional Organization**

NISW **National Institute for Social Work**

NJ postcode for **New Jersey**, a US state

NKVD **Narodny Komissariat Vnutrennikh Del** (Russian), People's Commissariat of Internal Affairs, the Soviet secret police 1934–38

NL *(Baseball) (US)* **National League**

NL **Netherlands**, international vehicle registration
NLC **National Labour Club**
NLF **National Liberal Federation**
NLLST **National Lending Library for Science and Technology**
NLP *(Computing)* **natural language processing**
NLP *(Psychotherapy)* **neurolinguistic programming**
NLQ *(Computing)* **near letter quality**
NLRB *(US)* **National Labor Relations Board**
NLS **National Library of Scotland**
NLW **National Library of Wales**
NLYL **National League of Young Liberals**
NM postcode for **New Mexico**, a US state
N. Mex. **New Mexico**, a US state
NMP *(Economics)* **net material product**
NMU **National Maritime Union**
NN postcode for **Northampton**
NNE **north-northeast**
NNEB **National Nursery Examination Board**
NNP *(Economics)* **net national product**
NNR **National Nature Reserve**
NNT **nuclear nonproliferation treaty**
NNW **north-northwest**
no. **number**
n.o. *(Cricket)* **not out**
No chemical symbol for **nobelium**
No. **number**
NO **naval officer**
NOC **National Olympic Committee**
NODA **National Operatic and Dramatic Association**
NODC **non-OPEC developing country**
n.o.k. **next of kin**
nom. *(Grammar)* **nominative**
Noncon. **Nonconformist**
NOP **National Opinion Poll**
NORAD **North American Air Defense Command**
Norf **Norfolk**, an English county
Northants **Northamptonshire**, an English county
Northd *or*
Northumb **Northumberland**, an English county
NORWEB **North Western Electricity Board**

Notar *or*
NOTAR **no-tail rotor** (aircraft)
NOTB **National Ophthalmic Treatment Board**
Notts **Nottinghamshire**, an English county
NOX **nitrogen oxide**
NOW *(US)* **National Organization for Women**
np **new paragraph**
np **new pence**
Np chemical symbol for **neptunium**
NP **National Party**, a South African right-of-centre political party
NP **National Power plc**
NP postcode for **Newport**
NP **Notary Public**
NPA **National Park Authority**
NPA **Newspaper Publishers' Association**
NPD **Nationaldemokratische Partei Deutschlands**, National Democratic Party of Germany, a neo-Nazi political party
NPFA **National Playing Fields Association**
NPG **National Portrait Gallery**
NPL **National Physical Laboratory**, a research establishment at Teddington, England
NPP **nuclear power plant**
NPS **nuclear power source**
NPS **nuclear power station**
NPT **nonproliferation treaty**
NPW **nuclear-powered warship**
NR postcode for **Norwich**
NRA *(US)* **National Recovery Administration**
NRA *(UK)* **National Rifle Association**
NRA **National Rifle Association of America**
NRA **National Rivers Authority**, the British agency responsible for managing water resources
NRC **National Research Council**
NRC *(US)* **Nuclear Regulatory Commission**
NRDC **National Research Development Corporation**
NRDS *(Medicine)* **neonatal respiratory distress syndrome**
NREM **non-rapid eye movement**
NROTC **Naval Reserve Officer Training Corps**
NRP **nuclear reprocessing plant**

NRPB **National Radiological Protection Board**
ns **nanosecond**
n/s **nonsmoker**; used in advertisements
NS **Newspaper Society**
NS **Nova Scotia**, a Canadian province
NS **nuclear ship**
NSA **National Security Agency**, the largest and most secret of US intelligence agencies, which intercepts foreign communications as well as safeguards US transmissions
NSA **National Skating Association**
NSAID **nonsteroidal anti-inflammatory drug, a drug used to relieve pain, for example in arthritis**
NSB **National Savings Bank**
NSC *(UK)* **National Safety Council**
NSC *(US)* **National Security Council**
NSC **National Sporting Club**
NSCR **National Society for Cancer Relief**
NSE **National Society for Epilepsy**
NSF *(US)* **National Science Foundation**
NSG **nonstatutory guidelines** (relating to the National Curriculum in schools)
NSHEB **North of Scotland Hydroelectric Board**
NSL **National Sporting League**
NSPCA *(US)* **National Society for the Prevention of Cruelty to Animals**
NSPCC *(UK)* **National Society for the Prevention of Cruelty to Children**
NSRA **National Smallbore Rifle Association**
NSU *(Medicine)* **nonspecific urethritis**
NSW **New South Wales**, an Australian state
NT **National Theatre**
NT **National Trust**
NT **New Testament**, the second part of the Bible, including the Gospels
NT **Northern Territory**, an Australian territory
NTB *(Economics)* **nontariff barrier**
NTDA **National Trade Development Association**
NTG **North Thames Gas**
NTP **normal temperature and pressure**, the former name for STP (standard temperature and pressure)

NTS **National Trust for Scotland**
NTVLRO **National Television Licence Records Office**
nt. wt. **net weight**
NUAAW **National Union of Agricultural and Allied Workers**
NUCPS **National Union of Civil and Public Servants**
NUCUA **National Union of Conservative and Unionist Associations**
NUI **National University of Ireland**
NUIW **National Union of Insurance Workers**
NUJ **National Union of Journalists**, a British trade union
NUJMB **Northern Universities Joint Matriculation Board**
Num **numbers**; used on a keyboard
Num. *(Bible)* **Numbers**
NUM **National Union of Mineworkers**, a British trade union
NUMAST **National Union of Marine, Aviation, and Shipping Transport Officers**, a British trade union
NUPE **National Union of Public Employees**, a British trade union
NUS **National Union of Students**, a British trade union
NUT **National Union of Teachers**, a British trade union
NUTG **National Union of Townswomen's Guilds**
NUTN **National Union of Trained Nurses**
NUU **New University of Ulster**
NV postcode for **Nevada**, a US state
NVG *(Military)* **night-vision goggles**
NVQ **National Vocational Qualification**, a certificate of attainment of a standardized level of skill and competence
NW **northwest**
NW postcode for **northwest London**
N-waste **nuclear waste**
n. wt. **net weight**
NWT **Northwest Territories**, a Canadian territory
NY postcode for **New York**, a US state
NY **New York**, a US city
NYC **New York City**
NYO **National Youth Orchestra**
NYOS **National Youth Orchestra of Scotland**
N. Yorks **North Yorkshire**, an English county
NYT **National Youth Theatre**
NZ **New Zealand**, international vehicle registration

O

O — **Ohio**, a US state
O — **Oregon**, a US state
O — chemical symbol for **oxygen**
o/a — **on account**
OAA — **Outdoor Advertising Association of Great Britain**
O & C — **Oxford and Cambridge** (Schools Examination Board)
OAO — **Orbiting Astronomical Observatory**
OAP — **old age pensioner**
OAPEC — **Organization of Arab Petroleum Exporting Countries**
OAS — **Organization of American States**, an association which aims to maintain peace and solidarity within the hemisphere
OASIS — **optimal aircraft sequencing using intelligent systems**
OAU — **Organization of African Unity**, established to eradicate colonialism and improve economic, cultural, and political cooperation in Africa
ob. — *obiit* (Latin), he died *or* she died
Ob — *(Bible)* **Obadiah**
OB — **outside broadcast**
Obad. — *(Bible)* **Obadiah**
OBE — **Officer of the Order of the British Empire**
OBE — **out-of-the-body experience**
obit. — **obituary**
Obogs — *(Military)* **on-board oxygen-generating system**
o/c *or* **OC** — **officer commanding**
OCA — **Old Comrades Association**
OCAM — **Organisation Commune Africaine et Mauricienne** (French), Joint African and Mauritian Organization, a body for economic cooperation in Africa
OCAS — **Organization of Central American States**
OCD — **obsessive compulsive disorder**
OCD — *(US)* **Office of Civil Defense**

OCF **Officiating Chaplain to the Forces**
OCR **optical character recognition** *or* **optical character reader**
OCS *(US)* **Officer Candidate School**
OCTU **Officer Cadet Training Unit**
OCU **Operational Conversion Unit**
o/d **overdrive**; used in car advertisements
OD ***oculus dexter*** (Latin), the right eye
OD *(US)* **officer of the day**
OD **olive drab**, the colour and material of US army uniforms
OD **overdose**
OD **overdrawn**
ODA **Overseas Development Administration**, a British government department responsible for the administration of development assistance to overseas countries
ODAS **Ocean Data Station**
ODESSA **Organisation der SS-Angehörigen** (German), Organization of SS members
ODI **Overseas Development Institute**
OE **Old English**
OEA **Overseas Education Association**
OECD **Organization for Economic Cooperation and Development**
OED **Oxford English Dictionary**
OEM *(Computing)* **original equipment manufacturer**
OEO **Office of Economic Opportunity**
OES **Order of the Eastern Star**
OF **Oddfellows**, members of the Independent Order of Oddfellows,
OFFER **Office of Electricity Regulation**
Ofgas *or* **OFGAS** **Office of Gas Supply**
OFS **Orange Free State**, a South African province
OFT **Office of Fair Trading**
Oftel *or* **OFTEL** **Office of Telecommunications**
Ofwat *or* **OFWAT** **Office of Water Services**
o.g. **own goal**
OGM **ordinary general meeting**

OGPU **Obedinyonnoye Gosudarstvennoye Polititcheskoye Upravleniye** (Russian), United State Political Administration, the Soviet secret police 1923–34
OH postcode for **Ohio**, a US state
OHMS **On Her/His Majesty's Service**
OHN **occupational health nurse**
OHP **overhead projector**
OHS **occupational health service**
OIC **officer in charge**
OIC **Organization of the Islamic Conference**, an international Muslim solidarity association
OJT **on-the-job training**
OK postcode for **Oklahoma**, a US state
Okla. **Oklahoma**, a US state
OL ***oculus laevus*** (Latin), the left eye
OL postcode for **Oldham**
OL *(Computing)* **on-line**, a system that allows the computer to work interactively with its users, responding to each instruction as it is given, as opposed to a batch system
OLE *(Computing)* **object linking and embedding**
O level **Ordinary level**, an examination taken by 16-year-olds, replaced by the GCSE in 1988
OLTP *(Computing)* **on-line transaction processing**
OM **Order of Merit**, a British order of chivalry that ranks below a knighthood
OMB *(US)* **Office of Management and Budget**
OMC **operation and maintenance costs**
OMCS **Office of the Minister for the Civil Service**
OMO **one-man operator** (of buses)
OMOV **one member, one vote**
ON **Ontario**, a Canadian province
ONC **Ordinary National Certificate**
o.n.o. **or nearest offer**; used on prices for goods being sold privately
Ont. **Ontario**, a Canadian province
OOD *(Computing)* **object-oriented design**
OOD **officer of the day**
OOL *(Computing)* **object-oriented language**
OOP *(Computing)* **object-oriented programming**
OOW **officer of the watch**

op. *opera* (Latin), works
op. *opus* (Latin), a work
Op. *(Music)* **Opus**
OP *(Military)* **observation post**
op-amp *(Electronics)* **operational amplifier**
op art **optical art**, a movement in modern art that uses optical effects to confuse the spectator's eye
OPAS **Occupational Pensions Advisory Service**
OPB **Occupational Pensions Board**
op. cit. *opere citato* (Latin), in the work cited; used in reference citations
OPCON **operational control**
OPCS **Office of Population Censuses and Surveys**
OPEC **Organization of Petroleum-Exporting Countries**, a body that coordinates price and supply policies of oil-producing states. Members are Algeria, Ecuador, Gabon, Indonesia, Iran, Iraq, Kuwait, Libya, Nigeria, Qatar, Saudi Arabia, United Arab Emirates and Venezuela.
Op-Ed **opposite-editorial page**, a page in a newspaper containing signed articles by commentators
OPEX **operational, executive, and administrative personnel**, in the United Nations
OPO **one-person operator** (of buses)
opp. **opposite**
OPP **oriented polypropene**, used to make a packaging film
OR **official receiver**
OR **operating room**
OR postcode for **Oregon**, a US state
Oracle **optional reception of announcements by coded line electronics**, the teletext system operated in the UK by Independent Television
Ore. *or* **Oreg.** **Oregon**, a US state
ORL **otorhinolaryngology**, the medical specialty concerned with the ear, nose, and throat
OROM *(Computing)* **optical read-only memory**
ORS **Operational Research Society**
Os chemical symbol for **osmium**
OS *oculus sinister* (Latin), the left eye
OS *(Computing)* **operating system**
OS **Ordinary Seaman**

OS — **Ordnance Survey**, the official body responsible for the mapping of Britain
OS — **outsize**; used on clothing labels
OSCAR — **Orbital Satellites Carrying Amateur Radio**
OSCAR — **Organization for Sickle Cell Anaemia Research**
OSE — **operational support equipment**
OSF — *(Computing)* **Open Software Foundation**
OSO — **orbiting solar observatory**
OST — *(US)* **Office of Science and Technology**
OSUK — **Ophthalmological Society of the United Kingdom**
OT — **occupational therapy**
OT — **Old Testament**
OT — **operating theatre**
OT — **overtime**
OTB — **off-track betting**, a system of legalized betting on horses, away from the racetrack
OTC — **Officers' Training Corps**
OTC — **one-stop inclusive tour charter**
OTC — **Organization for Trade Cooperation**
OTC — **over-the-counter**, as in the selling of medicines
OTE — **on-target earnings**; used in job advertisements
OTS — **officer training school**
OTU — **operational training unit**
OU — **Open University**
OU — **Oxford University**
OUP — **Official (Ulster) Unionist Party**, a Northern Irish moderate right-of-centre political party
OUP — **Oxford University Press**
OX — postcode for **Oxford**
Oxbridge — **Oxford and Cambridge** (universities)
OXFAM — **Oxford Committee for Famine Relief**, a charity that works to relieve poverty and famine worldwide
Oxon — **Oxfordshire**, an English county
oz — symbol for **ounce**

P

p	**page**
p	**penny** *or* **pence**
p	*(Music)* ***piano*** (Italian), softly
p	**proton**
p.	*(Baseball)* **pitcher**
P	**parking**; used on road signs
P	*(Chess)* **pawn**
P	chemical symbol for **phosphorus**
P	**Portugal**, international vehicle registration
P	**Post Office**; used on maps
P	**President**
p.a.	***per annum*** (Latin), yearly
Pa	symbol for **pascal**, unit of pressure
Pa	chemical symbol for **protactinium**
Pa.	**Pennsylvania**, a US state
PA	postcode for **Paisley**
PA	**Panama**, international vehicle registration
PA	postcode for **Pennsylvania**, a US state
PA	**Piper Aircraft**, e.g. the PA-28
PA	**Press Association**
PA	**public address** (system)
PA	**Publishers' Association**
PABX	*(Telephony)* **private automatic branch exchange**
PAC	**Pan-African Congress**, a militant black South African nationalist group
PAC	**political action committee**, any US organization that raises funds for political candidates
PAC	**Public Accounts Committee**
PACE	**Police and Criminal Evidence Act**
pact *or* PACT	**Producers' Alliance for Cinema and Television**
PAD	**passive air defence**
PAGB	**Proprietary Association of Great Britain**

PAL	*(Television)* **phase alternation line**
P and L *or* **P & L**	**profit and loss**
P & O	**Peninsular and Oriental Steamship Company**
p & p	**postage and packing**
par.	**paragraph**
PAR	*(Military)* **perimeter acquisition radar**
PAR	**phased-array radar**
PAR	*(Aeronautics)* **precision approach radar**
para.	**paragraph**
paren.	**parenthesis**
Parl.	**Parliament**
part.	**participle**
pas	**power-assisted steering**; used in car advertisements
PAS	**public-address system**
Pascal *or* **PASCAL**	*(Computing)* ***program appliqué à la selection et la compilation automatique de la littérature*** (French), a high-level programming language
PASOK	**Panellinion Socialistikon Kinema**, Panhellenic Socialist Movement, a Greek democratic socialist political party
pass.	**(Grammar) passive**
PAT	**Professional Association of Teachers**, a British trade union
Pat. Off.	**Patent Office**
pat. pend.	**patent pending**
PAX	*(Telephony)* **private automatic exchange**
PAYE	**pay as you earn**, a system of tax collection
PAYV	**pay as you view**
Pb	chemical symbol for **lead**
PBB	**polybrominated biphenyl**, a toxic industrial chemical
PBS	**Public Broadcasting Service**, a US television network
PBX	*(Telephony)* **private branch exchange**
pc.	**piece**
p.c.	**per cent**
p.c.	***post cibos*** (Latin), after meals; used in prescriptions
PC	**Panama Canal**
PC	**Parish Council**
PC	**Peace Corps**, a US organization that sends skilled people to work in developing countries
PC	**personal computer**

PC	**Plaid Cymru** (Welsh), Party of Wales, a Welsh nationalist political party
PC	**Police Constable**
PC	**political correctness** *or* **politically correct**
PC	**printed circuit**
pcb	**printed circuit board**
PCB	**polychlorinated biphenyl**, one of a group of dangerous industrial chemicals
PCB	**printed circuit board**
PCC	**Press Complaints Commission**, a British organization that works to preserve the freedom of the press
PCE	**Postgraduate Certificate of Education**
pcf	**pounds per cubic foot**
PCF	**Parti Communiste Français**, French Communist Party
PCFC	**Polytechnics and Colleges Funding Council**
pci	**pounds per cubic inch**
PCL	*(Computing)* **printer control language**
pcm	**per calendar month**
PCM	*(Physics, Telecommunications)* **pulse-code modulation**
PCN	*(Computing)* **personal communications network**
PCOD	**polycystic ovary disease**
PCP	**pentachlorophenol**, a wood preservative
PCP	**phencyclohexyl-piperidine**, a powerful hallucinogenic drug, also known as angel dust
PCP	*(Medicine)* **pneumocystis carinii pneumonia**
pcs.	**pieces**
PCS	**Parti Chrétien Social** (French), Christian Social Party, a Luxembourg moderate left-of-centre political party
PCTE	*(Computing)* **portable common tool environment**
Pd	chemical symbol for **palladium**
PD	*(US)* **Police Department**
PD	**Progressive Democrat**, a member of the Irish Progressive Democratic party
PD	*(Computing)* **public domain** (software)
PDA	*(Computing)* **personal digital assistant**
PDGF	**platelet-derived growth factor**
PDL	*(Computing)* **page description language**
PDL	**Parti Democratique Luxembourgeois** (French), Luxembourg Democratic Party, a Luxembourg centre-left political party

PDM **physical distribution management**
PDN **public data network**
PDS **Parkinson's Disease Society**
PDS **Partei des Demokratischen Sozialismus**, Party of Democratic Socialism, a German reform-communist political party
PDSA **People's Dispensary for Sick Animals**
PDT *(US)* **Pacific Daylight Time**
PE **Peru**, international vehicle registration
PE postcode for **Peterborough**
PE *(Computing)* **phase-encoded** (tape)
PE **physical education**
PE **Protestant Episcopal**
PEA **Physical Education Association of Great Britain and Northern Ireland**
PEI **Prince Edward Island**, a Canadian province
PEN **Poets, Playwrights, Editors, Essayists, Novelists**, a literary association that promotes international understanding among writers
Penn. **Pennsylvania**, a US state
Pep *or* **PEP** **personal equity plan**, an investment scheme
PERA **Production Engineering Research Association of Great Britain**
per pro. ***per procurationem*** (Latin), by proxy; used when signing a letter on someone else's behalf
PERT **programme** (*or* **project**) **evaluation and review technique**, a technique used in project management
PEST **Pressure for Economic and Social Toryism**, a left-wing group within the Conservative party
Pet. *(Bible)* **Peter**
PET **polyethylene terephthalate**, a plastic used for packaging food
PET **positron emission tomography**, a medical scanning technique involving the injection or inhalation of a radioactive chemical
PETN **pentaerythritol tetranitrate**, an explosive
PETRAS **Polytechnic Educational Technology Resources Advisory Service**
pF *(Physics)* **picofarad**
PF **Procurator Fiscal**

PFA **Professional Footballers' Association**
PFC **polychlorinated fluorocarbon**
PFC *(US)* **Private First Class**
PFLP **Popular Front for the Liberation of Palestine**
PG **parental guidance**, a film classification
PGA **Professional Golfers' Association**
PGCE **Postgraduate Certificate of Education**, a British teaching qualification
PG Cert **Postgraduate Certificate**
PG Dip **Postgraduate Diploma**
PgDn **page down**; used on a keyboard
PGF **polypeptide growth factor**
PGL *(Medicine)* **persistent generalized lymphadenopathy**
PGM **precision-guided missile**
PgUp **page up**; used on a keyboard
pH **potential of hydrogen ions**, used as a scale for measuring acidity or alkalinity
Ph *or* **Ph.** **Philosophy**; used in degrees
PH postcode for **Perth**
PH **public health**
PHAB **Physically Handicapped and Able-Bodied**, a British charitable organization furthering the integration of people with and without physical disabilities
PHC **Pharmaceutical Chemist**
PHC **primary health care**
PhD ***Philosophiae Doctor*** (Latin), Doctor of Philosophy
PHE **Public Health Engineer**
PHF **pulsed high frequency**, the use of radio waves to heal damaged tissue in the body
Phil. **Philadelphia**, a US state
Phil. **Philharmonic**
Phil. *(Bible)* **Philippians**
Philem. *(Bible)* **Philemon**
PHLS **Public Health Laboratory Service**
phys. ed. **physical education**
PI **parainfluenza virus**
PI **private investigator**
PIA **Pakistan International Airlines Corporation**
PIA **Partitioning Industry Association**
PIA **Personal Investment Authority**

PIBOR **Paris Interbank Offered Rate**
PIC *(Computing)* **programmable interrupt controller**
PID **pelvic inflammatory disease**
PID *(Computing)* **personal identification device**
PID **prolapsed intervertebral disc** (a slipped disc)
PIDS *(Medicine)* **primary immune deficiency syndrome**
PIH *(Medicine)* **pregnancy-induced hypertension**
PIK **payment in kind**
pil. ***pilula*** (Latin), pill; used in prescriptions
PILL *(Computing)* **programmed instruction language learning**
PIM *(Computing)* **personal information manager**
PIMS **profit impact of marketing strategy**
PIN **personal identification number**; used to make transactions using cash or credit cards
pinx. ***pinxit*** (Latin), he or she painted it
PIRA **Paper Industries Research Association**
pixel **picture element**, a single dot on a computer screen
p.j.'s *(US)* **pyjamas**
PK **Pakistan**, international vehicle registration
PK test *(Medicine)* **Prausnitz-Kustner test**
pkwy. **parkway**
Pl **Place**; used in street names
PL **Paymaster Lieutenant**
PL postcode for **Plymouth**
PL **Poland**, international vehicle registration
PL *(Computing)* **programming language**
PLA **People's Liberation Army**, China's national army
PLA **Port of London Authority**
Plato *or* **PLATO** *(Computing)* **programmed logic for automatic teaching operation**
plc *or* **PLC** **public limited company**
PLM **Paris-Lyons-Mediterranean** (railway)
PL/M *(Computing)* **Programming Language for Microcomputers**
PLO **Palestine Liberation Organization**, an Arab organization founded to bring about an independent state of Palestine
PLP **Parliamentary Labour Party**
PLR **public lending right**, a method of paying a royalty to

authors when books are borrowed from libraries

PLSS **personal** (*or* **portable**) **life-support system**, used by astronauts

Pluna *or* **PLUNA** **Primeras Líneas Uruguayas de Navegación Aérea**, Uruguayan airline

plur. *(Grammar)* **plural**

PL/Z *(Computing)* **Programming Language Zilog**

p.m. ***post meridiem*** (Latin), after noon

p.m. **postmortem** (examination)

Pm chemical symbol for **promethium**

PM ***post meridiem*** (Latin), after noon

PM **postmortem** (examination)

PM **Prime Minister**

PM **Provost Marshal**

PMA **paramethoxyamphetamine**, a hallucinogenic drug

PMA **polymethyl acrylate**, a synthetic polymer

PMBX *(Telephony)* **private manual branch exchange**

PMC **Personnel Management Centre**

PMG **Paymaster General**

PMG **Postmaster General**

PMG **Provost Marshal General**

PMH **previous medical history**

PMO **Principal Medical Officer**

PMS **premenstrual syndrome**, a medical condition caused by hormone changes occurring cyclically before menstruation

PMT **premenstrual tension**, another name for PMS

PMX *(Telephony)* **private manual exchange**

PN **postnatal**

PN *(Computing)* **pseudo-noise**

P/N **postnatal**

PNA **Psychiatric Nurses Association**

PNdB **perceived noise decibel**

PNEU **Parents' National Education Union**

PNG **Papua New Guinea**, international vehicle registration

PNS **parasympathetic nervous system**

PNV **Partido Nacional Vasco**, Basque National Party

pnxt ***pinxit*** (Latin), he or she painted it

p.o. ***per os*** (Latin), by mouth; used in prescriptions

Po chemical symbol for **polonium**

PO **parole officer**
PO **personnel officer**
PO **petty officer**
PO **Philharmonic Orchestra**
PO postcode for **Portsmouth**
PO **postal order**
PO **Post Office**
POA **Prison Officers' Association**, a British trade union
POB **Post Office Box**
p.o.c. *or*
POC **port of call**
POD **pay on delivery**
POD **port of debarkation**
POE **port of embarkation**
POE **port of entry**
POEU **Post Office Engineers Union**
P. of W. **Prince of Wales**
POGO **Polar Orbiting Geophysical Observatory**
POL **petroleum, oil, and lubricants**
POM **prescription-only medicine**
p.o.r. **pay on receipt**
p.o.r. **pay on return**
POS **point of sale**, such as a supermarket checkout
POSL **Parti Ouvrier Socialiste Luxembourgeois** (French), Luxembourg Socialist Workers' Party, a moderate socialist political party
poss. *(Grammar)* **possessive**
POSSLQ **person of the opposite sex sharing living quarters**
POST **Parliamentary Office of Science and Technology**
POST **point-of-sales terminal**
POUNC **Post Office Users' National Council**
POW **Prince of Wales**
POW **prisoner of war**
pp *(Music)* ***pianissimo*** (Italian), very quietly
pp. **pages**
pp *or* **p.p.** ***per procurationem*** (Latin), by proxy; used when signing a letter on someone else's behalf
p.p. **post paid**
p.p. ***post prandium*** (Latin), after a meal; used in prescriptions
PP **parcel post**

PP **parish priest**
PP **Partido Popular**, Popular Party, a Spanish right-wing political party
PPA **Periodical Publishers' Association**
PPA **Pre-School Playgroups Association**
ppb **parts per billion**
PPC **progressive patient care**
PPE **philosophy, politics, and economics**, a university course
PPH **post-partum haemorrhage**
PPITB **Printing and Publishing Industry Training Board**
ppm **pages per minute**
ppm **parts per million**
ppm **pulse per minute**
PPM *(Electronics)* **peak programme meter**
PPMA **Produce Packaging and Marketing Association**
PPN *(Computing)* **public packet network**
ppp *(Music)* ***pianississimo*** (Italian), as quietly as possible
PPP **Pakistan People's Party**, a political party advocating democracy and Islamic socialism
PPP **personal pension plan**
PPR **printed paper rate** (for postage)
PPS **Parliamentary Private Secretary**
PPS **pelvic pain syndrome**
PPU **Peace Pledge Union**
PQ **parliamentary question**
PQ **Province of Quebec**, Canada
p.r. ***per rectum*** (Latin), by the rectum; used in prescriptions
Pr chemical symbol for **praseodymium**
PR **parliamentary report**
PR postcode for **Preston**
PR **proportional representation**, an electoral system
PR **public relations**
PR **Puerto Rico**, an island in the Greater Antilles
PRA *(US)* **Public Roads Administration**
PRB **Pre-Raphaelite Brotherhood**, a group of British painters 1848–53
PRC **People's Republic of China**
PRD **Partido Renovador Democrático**, Democratic Renewal Party, a Portuguese centre-left political party
pref. **prefix**

Pres. *or*
Presb. **Presbyterian**
pret. *(Grammar)* **preterite**
PRF *(Electronics)* **pulse repetition (*or* recurrence) frequency**
PRI **Plastics and Rubber Institute**
PRL **Parti Réformateur Libéral** (French), Liberal Reform Party, a Belgian moderate centrist political party
p.r.n. ***pro re nata*** (Latin), as occasion arises; used in prescriptions
PRO **Public Record Office**
PRO **public relations officer**
Proc. **Proceedings**
Prof. **Professor**
prog. **program**
Prog. **Progressive**
Prolog *or*
PROLOG *(Computing)* **programming in logic**, a language used in artificial intelligence
PROM *(Computing)* **programmable read-only memory**
pron. **pronoun**
PROP **Preservation of the Rights of Prisoners**
propr **proprietor**
Prot. **Protestant**
pro tem. ***pro tempore*** (Latin), for the time being
Prov. *(Bible)* **Proverbs**
Prov. **Province**
PRP **performance-related pay**
PRP **profit-related pay**
PRS **Performing Rights Society**
ps **picosecond**
ps **postscript**
Ps. *(Bible)* **Psalms**
PS **Parliamentary Secretary**
PS **Partido Socialista**, Socialist Party, a Portuguese progressive socialist political party
PS **Parti Socialiste** (French), Socialist Party, a Belgian left-of-centre political party
PS **Pastel Society**
PS **Permanent Secretary**
PS **Police Sergeant**

PS **postscript**
Psa. *(Bible)* **Psalms**
PSA **Property Services Agency**
PSA *(Medicine)* **prostatic specific antigen**
PSBR **public sector borrowing requirement**, the amount of money needed by a government to cover any deficit in financing its own activities
PSC **Parti Social Chrétien** (French), Christian Social Party, a Belgian centre-left political party, also known as Christelijke Volkspartij (Flemish)
PSD **Partido Social Democrata**, Social Democratic Party, a Portuguese moderate left-of-centre political party
PSDR **public sector debt repayment**, the amount left over when government expenditure is subtracted from receipts
PSE **Pacific Stock Exchange**
psf *or* **p.s.f.** **pounds per square foot**
PSFD **public sector financial deficit**
PSHFA **Public Servants Housing Finance Association**
psi *or* **p.s.i.** **pounds per square inch**
PSI **Policy Standards Institute**
psia **pounds per square inch, absolute**
psid **pounds per square inch, differential**
psig **pounds per square inch, gauge**
PSK **phase-shift keying**
PSL *(Economics)* **private-sector liquidity**
PSL **public-sector loan**
PSNC **Pacific Steam Navigation Company**
PSO **Principal Scientific Officer**
PSOE **Partido Socialista Obrero Español**, Spanish Socialist Workers' Party, a democratic socialist political party
PSS *(Computing)* **Packet Switch Stream**
PSSC **Personal Social Services Council**
PST *(US)* **Pacific Standard Time**
PSTN *(Telephony)* **public switched telephone network**
PSV **public service vehicle**
PSW **psychiatric social worker**
pt **pint**
pt **point**
p.t. **part time**
p.t. **past tense**

Pt chemical symbol for **platinum**
Pt **Point**; used in place names
Pt **Port**; used in place names
PT *(US)* **Pacific Time**
PT **physical therapy**
PT **physical training**
PTA **Parent-Teacher Association**
PTA **Passenger Transport Authority**
PT boat **patrol torpedo boat**
PTC *(Medicine)* **percutaneous transhepatic cholangiography**
PTCA *(Medicine)* **percutaneous transluminal coronary angioplasty**
Pte *(Military)* **Private**
Pte *(India)* **private limited company**; used after company names
PTE **Passenger Transport Executive**
PTFE **polytetrafluoroethylene**, a thermosetting plastic used to produce non-stick surfaces on pans
PTI *(Computing)* **public tool interface**
PTM **pulse-time modulation**
PTN **public telephone network**
PTN **public transportation network**
pto *or* **PTO** **please turn over**
PTO **power takeoff**
PTO **Public Trustee Office**
pts **parts**
pts **pints**
pts **points**
PTS **Philatelic Traders' Society**
PTSD **post-traumatic stress disorder**
PTT **Postal, Telegraph, and Telephone Administration**
PTV **public television**
Pty *(Australia, South Africa)* **Proprietary**; used after company names
Pu chemical symbol for **plutonium**
PU **polyurethane**
PUO **pyrexia of unknown origin** (fever)
PUVA **psoralen ultraviolet A**, a treatment for psoriasis, a skin disease
p.v. ***per vaginam*** (Latin), by the vagina; used on prescriptions

PV	*petite vitesse* (French), goods or slow train
PVA	**polyvinyl acetate**
PVA	**polyvinyl alcohol**
PVC	**polyvinyl chloride**, a type of plastic; used for drainpipes, audio discs, and shoes, for example
PVD	**peripheral vascular disease**
PvdA	**Partij van de Arbeid van België** (Flemish), Labour Party, a Belgian moderate left-of-centre political party
PVF	**polyvinyl fluoride**
PVP	**polyvinyl pyrrolidone**
PVS	**persistent vegetative state**
PVS	*(Medicine)* **postviral syndrome**, another name for ME
Pvt	*(Military)* **Private**
PVV	**Partij voor Vrijheid en Vooruitgang** (Flemish), Liberal Party, a Belgian moderate centrist political party
pw *or* **p.w.**	**per week**
PW	**policewoman**
PW	**public works**
PWA	**person with AIDS**
PWD	**Public Works Department**
PWE	**Political Welfare Executive**
PWLB	**Public Works Loan Board**
PWR	**pressurized water reactor**, a nuclear reactor design
pwt	**pennyweight**
px	**Pedro Ximénez**, a grape used in sweet wines and sherries
PX	**Post Exchange**, a US organization that provides shopping and canteen facilities for armed forces at home and abroad
PX	*(Telephony)* **private exchange**
P/X	**part exchange**; used in advertisements
pxt	***pinxit*** (Latin), he or she painted it
PY	**Paraguay**, international vehicle registration
pyo *or* **PYO**	**pick your own**; used on farm signs
PZI	**protamine zinc insulin**

Q

Q	*(Chess)* **queen**
Q	**queen**; used on playing cards
QA	**quality assurance**
QAM	*(Telecommunications)* **quadrature amplitude modulation**
Qantas	**Queensland and Northern Territory Aerial Service**, the Australian national airline
QB	**Queen's Bench**
QBD	**Queen's Bench Division**
QC	**quality control**
QC	**Quartermaster Corps**
QC	**Queen's Counsel**, a barrister in England appointed to senior rank by the Lord Chancellor
QCD	*(Physics)* **quantum chromodynamics**, a theory that describes the interaction of quarks
q. d.	***quaque die*** (Latin), every day; used in prescriptions
q.d.s.	***quater in die sumendus*** (Latin), to be taken four times a day; used in prescriptions
QED	*(Physics)* **quantum electrodynamics**, a theory that combines quantum theory and relativity
QED	***quod erat demonstrandum*** (Latin), which was to be proved; used after a proof
QEH	**Queen Elizabeth Hall**, in London
QF	**quick-firing**
QFD	*(Physics)* **quantum flavourdynamics**
QGM	**Queen's Gallantry Medal**
q.h.	***quaque hora*** (Latin), every hour; used in prescriptions
QI	**quartz-iodine**
q.i.d.	***quater in die*** (Latin), four times a day; used in prescriptions
QISAM	*(Computing)* **queued indexed sequential access method**
ql	**quintal**
q.l.	***quantum libet*** (Latin), as much as you like; used in prescriptions

QL	*(Computing)* **query language**
Qld *or* **QLD**	**Queensland**, an Australian state
q.m.	***quaque mane*** (Latin), every morning; used in prescriptions
QM	*(Physics)* **quantum mechanics**
QM	**Quartermaster**
QMG	**Quartermaster-General**
Qmr	**Quartermaster**
QMS	**Quartermaster-Sergeant**
q.n.	***quaque nocte*** (Latin), every night; used in prescriptions
QO	**qualified officer**
Q(ops)	**Quartering (operations)**
q.p. *or* **q.pl.**	***quantum placet*** (Latin), as much as seems good; used in prescriptions
QPR	**Queen's Park Rangers** (football club)
qq. hor.	***quaque hora*** (Latin), every hour; used in prescriptions
q.s.	***quantum sufficit*** (Latin), as much as necessary; used in prescriptions
QS	**quadrophonic-stereophonic**
QS	**quantity surveyor**
QSO	**quasi-stellar object** (a quasar)
QSS	**quasi-stellar source**
QSTOL	**quiet takeoff and landing**
qtr	**quarter**
quango	**quasi-autonomous non-governmental organization**
quasar	**quasi-stellar object**, a class of starlike celestial objects far beyond our galaxy
Que.	**Quebec**, a Canadian province
qv	***quod vide*** (Latin), which see; used when cross-referring in an encyclopedia, for example

R

r	symbol for **roentgen**, a unit of radiation exposure
r.	*(Baseball, Cricket)* **run** *or* **runs**
R	**Republican**
R	*(Physics)* **resistance**
R	**restricted**, a film classification
R	**River**
R	*(Chess)* **rook**
Ra	chemical symbol for **radium**
RA	**Argentina**, international vehicle registration
RA	**Rear-Admiral**
RA	*(US)* **Regular Army**
RA	**Royal Academy (the Royal Academy of Arts)**
RA	**Royal Artillery**
RAA	**Royal Academy of Arts**, a British society founded in 1768 to encourage artists
RAAF	**Royal Australian Air Force**
RAAF	**Royal Auxiliary Airforce**
RABDF	**Royal Association of British Dairy Farmers**
RABI	**Royal Agricultural Benevolent Institution**
RAC	**Royal Agricultural College**
RAC	**Royal Armoured Corps**
RAC	**Royal Automobile Club**, a British motoring organization
RACE	**Research and Development in Advanced Communication Technologies for Europe**
rad	symbol for **radian**, unit of measurement for plane angles
rad.	**radiator**
RAD	**Royal Academy of Dancing**
RADA	**Royal Academy of Dramatic Art**, a college in London where young actors are trained
radar	**radio direction and ranging**
RADAR	**Royal Association for Disability and Rehabilitation**
RADIUS	**Religious Drama Society of Great Britain**

RAdm *or*
RADM **Rear-Admiral**
RAE **Royal Aerospace Establishment**
RAeS **Royal Aeronautical Society**
RAF **Royal Air Force**
RAFA **Royal Air Forces Association**
RAFBF **Royal Air Force Benevolent Fund**
RAFG **Royal Air Force Germany**
RAFRO **Royal Air Force Reserve of Officers**
RAFVR **Royal Air Force Volunteer Reserve**
RAI **Radiotelevisione Italiana**, Italian broadcasting corporation
RAI **Royal Anthropological Institute**
r.a.m. **relative atomic mass**
RAM *(Computing)* **random-access memory**
RAM **Royal Academy of Music**, a music school in London
RAMC **Royal Army Medical Corps**
RAN **Royal Australian Navy**
r & b *or*
R & B **rhythm and blues**
R & D **research and development**, a process undertaken by a business organization before the launch of a product
R and R *(Medicine)* **rescue and resuscitation**
R and R **rest and recreation** *or* **rest and recuperation**
R & R *(Medicine)* **rescue and resuscitation**
R & R **rest and recreation** *or* **rest and recuperation**
R & R **rock and roll**
R & VA **Rating and Valuation Association**
RAOB **Royal Antediluvian Order of Buffaloes**
RAOC **Royal Army Ordnance Corps**
RAP **Regimental Aid Post**
RAPC **Royal Army Pay Corps**
RAPID **Register for the Ascertainment and Prevention of Inherited Diseases**
RARDE **Royal Armament Research and Development Establishment**
RARO **Regular Army Reserve of Officers**
RAS **Royal Agricultural Society**
RAS **Royal Asiatic Society**
RAS **Royal Astronomical Society**

RASE **Royal Agricultural Society of England**
RATO **rocket-assisted takeoff**
RAuxAF **Royal Auxiliary Air Force**
RAVC **Royal Army Veterinary Corps**
RAX *(Telephony)* **rural automatic exchange**
Rb chemical symbol for **rubidium**
RB **Republic of Botswana**, international vehicle registration
RB **Rifle Brigade**
RB **Royal Ballet**
RBA **Royal Society of British Artists**
RBE **relative biological effectiveness**, the relative damage caused to living tissue by different types of radiation
r/belts **rear seatbelts**; used in car advertisements
R.B.I. *(Baseball)* **run** *or* **runs batted in**
RBNA **Royal British Nurses' Association**
RBS **Royal Society of British Sculptors**
RBT **random breath-testing**
RC **Red Cross**
RC **Reserve Corps**
RC **Roman Catholic**
RC **Taiwan**, international vehicle registration
RCA **Central African Republic**, international vehicle registration
RCA **Radio Corporation of America**
RCA **Royal College of Art**
RCAF **Royal Canadian Air Force**
RCB(CG) **Republic of the Congo**, international vehicle registration
RCD **Regional Cooperation for Development**, a tripartite agreement between Iran, Pakistan, and Turkey for closer economic, technical, and cultural cooperation
RCD **residual current device**, a device that protects users of electrical equipment from electric shock
RCDS **Royal College of Defence Studies**
RCGP **Royal College of General Practitioners**
RCH **Republic of Chile**, international vehicle registration
RCHM **Royal Commission on Historical Monuments**
RCM **radar countermeasures**
RCM **Royal College of Midwives**
RCM **Royal College of Music**, a college in London providing a full-time musical education
RCMP **Royal Canadian Mounted Police**

RCN	**Royal Canadian Navy**
RCN	**Royal College of Nursing**
RCO	**Royal College of Organists**
RCOG	**Royal College of Obstetricians and Gynaecologists**
RCP	**Royal College of Physicians**
RCPath	**Royal College of Pathologists**
RCPE	**Royal College of Physicians, Edinburgh**
RCPI	**Royal College of Physicians of Ireland**
RCPSG	**Royal College of Physicians and Surgeons of Glasgow**
RCPsych	**Royal College of Psychiatrists**
RCR	**Royal College of Radiologists**
RCS	**Royal College of Science**
RCS	**Royal College of Surgeons of England**
RCS	**Royal Commonwealth Society**
RCSB	**Royal Commonwealth Society for the Blind**
RCSE	**Royal College of Surgeons of Edinburgh**
RCSI	**Royal College of Surgeons in Ireland**
RCT	**remote control transmitter**
RCT	**Royal Corps of Transport**
RCVS	**Royal College of Veterinary Surgeons**
r.d.	**relative density**
Rd	**road**; used in street names
RD	***récemment dégorgé*** (French), recently disgorged; used with reference to wine
RD	**Royal Dragoons**
RDA	**recommended dietary** (*or* **daily**) **allowance**
RDA	**Royal Defence Academy**
RD & D	**research, development, and demonstration**
RD & E	**research, development, and engineering**
RDAT *or* **R-DAT**	**rotary-head digital audio tape**
RDB	*(Military)* **Research and Development Board**
RDBMS	*(Computing)* **relational database management system**
RDC	**Royal Defence Corps**
RDC	**Rural District Council**
RDF	**radio direction finder**
RDS	**radio data system**
RDS	**respiratory distress syndrome**, a condition in which a newborn baby's lungs are insufficiently expanded to permit adequate oxygenation

RDS	**Royal Drawing Society**
RDT & E	**research, development, testing, and engineering**
RDX	**Research Department Explosive**
Re	chemical symbol for **rhenium**
RE	**Reformed Episcopal**
RE	**religious education**
RE	**Royal Engineers**
RE	**Royal Exchange**
RE	**Royal Society of Painter-Etchers and Engravers**
REACH	**Retired Executives' Action Clearing House**
react	**research education and aid for children with potentially terminal illness**
Rear-Adm	**Rear-Admiral**
REC	**regional electric company**
REconS	**Royal Economic Society**
Rect.	**Rector** *or* **Rectory**
redox	**reduction-oxidation**
Red R	**Register of Engineers for Disaster Relief**
Ref. Ch.	**Reformed Church**
Ref. Pres.	**Reformed Presbyterian**
reg	**registration**; used in car advertisements
Reg-Gen	**Registrar-General**
Reg. Prof.	**Regius Professor**, the holder of a university position instituted by a monarch
REIT	**real-estate investment trust**
rel. pron.	**relative pronoun**
rem	**roentgen equivalent man**, a unit of radiation dose equivalent, superseded by sievert
REM	**rapid eye movement**, the phase of sleep associated with dreaming
REME	**Royal Electrical and Mechanical Engineers**
REN	*(Telecommunications)* **ringer equivalence number**
Rep.	*(US)* **Representative**
Rep.	**Republic**
Rep.	*(US)* **Republican**
REPC	**Regional Economic Planning Council**
repro.	**reproduction**
Repub.	*(US)* **Republican**
RERO	**Royal Engineers Reserve of Officers**
RES	**Royal Entmological Society of London**

Rev. *(Bible)* **Revelation**
Rev. **Reverend**
Rev. **Review**
Revd **Reverend**
Rev. Ver. **Revised Version**, of the Bible
r.f. *or* **RF** **radio frequency**
RFA **Royal Field Artillery**
RFA **Royal Fleet Auxiliary**
RFC **Royal Flying Corps**
RFC **Rugby Football Club**
RFH **Royal Festival Hall**, in London
RFI **radio-frequency interference**
RFS **Registry of Friendly Societies**
RFS **Royal Forestry Society**
RFU **Rugby Football Union**
RG postcode for **Reading**
RGA **Royal Garrison Artillery**
RGB *(Engineering)* **red, green, blue**
RGG **Royal Grenadier Guards**
RGI **Royal Glasgow Institute of the Fine Arts**
RGJ **Royal Green Jackets**, a regiment of the British Army
RGN **Registered General Nurse**
RGNP **real gross national product**
RGO **Royal Greenwich Observatory**, the British astronomical observatory, transferred to Cambridge in 1990
RGS **Royal Geographical Society**
r.h. **right hand** *or* **right-handed**
Rh **rhesus** (factor)
Rh chemical symbol for **rhodium**
RH postcode for **Redhill**
RH **Republic of Haiti**, international vehicle registration
RH **right hand** *or* **right-handed**
RH **Royal Highness**
RHA **Regional Health Authority**
RHA **Road Haulage Association**
RHA **Royal Hibernian Academy**
RHA **Royal Horse Artillery**
RHAS **Royal Highland and Agricultural Society of Scotland**
RHB **Regional Hospital Board**
r.h.d. **right-hand drive**

RHHI **Royal Hospital and Home for Incurables**
RHistS **Royal Historical Society**
RHM **Rank Hovis McDougall**
RHS **Royal Historical Society**
RHS **Royal Horticultural Society**
RHS **Royal Humane Society**
RHV **Registered Health Visitor**
RI **Railway Inspectorate**
RI **religious instruction**
RI **Republic of Indonesia**, international vehicle registration
RI postcode for **Rhode Island**, a US state
RI **Rotary International**
RI **Royal Institution of Great Britain**, an organization for the promotion, diffusion, and extension of science and knowledge
RIA **Royal Irish Academy**
RIAA **Recording Industry Association of America**
RIAI **Royal Institute of the Architects of Ireland**
RIAS **Royal Incorporation of Architects in Scotland**
RIB **rigid-hull inflatable boat**
Riba *or*
RIBA **Royal Institute of British Architects**
RIC **Royal Irish Constabulary**
RICA **Research Institute for Consumer Affairs**
RICS **Royal Institution of Chartered Surveyors**
RIF *(Military)* **reduction in force**
RIFF **resource interchange file format**
RIIA **Royal Institute of International Affairs**
RIM **Islamic Republic of Mauritania**, international vehicle registration
RIMNET **Radioactive Incident Monitoring Network**, a network at Meteorological Office sites around the UK to record contamination levels
RINA **Royal Institution of Naval Architects**
RIOP **Royal Institution of Oil Painters**
RIP *(Computing)* **raster input processor**
RIP ***requiescat in pace*** (Latin), may he or she rest in peace
RIPA **Royal Institute of Public Administration**
RIPH & H *or*
RIPHH **Royal Institute of Public Health and Hygiene**

RISC *(Computing)* **reduced instruction-set computer**, a microprocessor
RJ **road junction**
RK **radical keratotomy**, a treatment for shortsightedness
RK **religious knowledge**
RKO **Radio Keith Orpheum**, a US film production and distribution company
RL **Republic of Lebanon**, international vehicle registration
RLO **returned letter office**
RLPO **Royal Liverpool Philharmonic Orchestra**
RLPS **Royal Liverpool Philharmonic Society**
RLSS **Royal Life Saving Society**
RM **Madagascar**, international vehicle registration
RM **Registered Midwife**
RM postcode for **Romford**
RM **Royal Mail**
RM **Royal Marines**, the British military force trained for amphibious warfare
RMA **Royal Marine Artillery**
RMA **Royal Military Academy**, the British officer training college at Sandhurst
RMA **Royal Musical Association**
RMCM **Royal Manchester College of Music**
RMCS **Royal Military College of Science**
RMetS **Royal Meteorological Society**
RMFVR **Royal Marine Forces Volunteer Reserve**
r.m.m. **relative molecular mass**
RMM **Republic of Mali**, international vehicle registration
RMN **Registered Mental Nurse**
RMO **resident medical officer**
RMP **Royal Military Police**
RMPA **Royal Medico-Psychological Association**
rms *or* **RMS** *(Maths)* **root mean square**
RMS **Royal Mail Service**
RMS **Royal Mail Ship** (*or* **Steamer**)
RMS **Royal Microscopical Society**
RMT **National Union of Rail, Maritime, and Transport Workers**, a British trade union
Rn chemical symbol for **radon**
RN *(US)* **Registered Nurse**

RN Republic of the Niger, international vehicle registration
RN **Royal Navy**
RNA **ribonucleic acid**, a nucleic acid involved in the process of translating the genetic material DNA into proteins
RNA **Royal Naval Association**
RNAS **Royal Naval Air Service**
RNAS **Royal Naval Air Station**
rNase *or* RNAse **ribonuclease**
RNBT **Royal Naval Benevolent Fund**
RNC **Royal Naval College**
RNCM **Royal Northern College of Music**
RND **Royal Naval Division**
RNIB **Royal National Institute for the Blind**
RNID **Royal National Institute for the Deaf**
RNLI **Royal National Lifeboat Institution**
RNLO **Royal Naval Liaison Officer**
RNMDSF **Royal National Mission to Deep Sea Fishermen**
RNMH **Registered Nurse for the Mentally Handicapped**
RNR **Royal Naval Reserve**
RNS **Royal Numismatic Society**
RNSC **Royal Naval Staff College**
RNT **Royal National Theatre**
RNVR **Royal Naval Volunteer Reserve**
RNXS **Royal Naval Auxiliary Service**
RNZAF **Royal New Zealand Air Force**
RNZN **Royal New Zealand Navy**
r.o. *(Cricket)* **run out**
RO **Radio Orchestra**
RO **Romania**, international vehicle registration
RoA *or* ROA *(Education)* **record of achievement**
ROE **Royal Observatory, Edinburgh**
ROF **Royal Ordnance Factory**
ROK **Republic of Korea**, international vehicle registration
Rom. *(Bible)* **Romans**
ROM *(Computing)* **read-only memory**
Rom. Cath. **Roman Catholic**
RORC **Royal Ocean Racing Club**
ro-ro **roll-on, roll-off** (ferry)
ROSE *(Computing)* **Research Open Systems in Europe**

ROSLA raising of school-leaving age

Rospa *or*
RoSPA Royal Society for the Prevention of Accidents

ROTC Reserve Officers' Training Corps

ROU **Republic of Uruguay**, international vehicle registration

RP Received Pronunciation

RP recommended price

RP Reformed Presbyterian

RP **Regius Professor**, the holder of a university position instituted by a monarch

RP **Republic of the Philippines**, international vehicle registration

PR **Parti Républicain**, Republican Party, a French centre-right political party

RPB recognized professional body

RPE Reformed Protestant Episcopal

RPG *(Computing)* **report program generator**

RPG rocket-propelled grenade

RPG role-playing game

RPI **retail price index**, an indicator of variations in the cost of living

rpm revolutions per minute

RPM **retail price maintenance**, a rule applying to some goods such as books in Britain, which means that the seller cannot reduce the price

RPMS Royal Postgraduate Medical School

RPO Royal Philharmonic Orchestra

RPR **Rassemblement pour la République**, Rally for the Republic, a French neo-Gaullist conservative political party

rps revolutions per second

RPS Royal Philharmonic Society

RPS Royal Photographic Society

RPSGB Royal Pharmaceutical Society of Great Britain

rpt repeat

rpt report

RPV **remotely piloted vehicle**, a crewless mini-aircraft used for military surveillance and to select targets in battle

RQMS regimental quartermaster sergeant

RR *(US)* **railroad**

RR **Right Reverend**
RR *or* **R-R** **Rolls-Royce**
rRNA **ribosomal RNA**
RRP **recommended retail price**
RRF **Rapid Reaction Force**, any military unit that is maintained at a high state of readiness to react to an emergency
RS **respiratory system**
RS **Royal Society**
RSA **Republic of South Africa**
RSA **Royal Scottish Academy**
RSA **Royal Society for the Encouragement of Arts, Manufactures, and Commerce**
RSA **Royal Society of Arts**
RSAMD **Royal Scottish Academy of Music and Drama**
RSC **Royal Shakespeare Company**, a professional theatre company that performs in Stratford and London
RSC **Royal Society of Canada**
RSC **Royal Society of Chemistry**
RSCM **Royal School of Church Music**
RSCN **Registered Sick Children's Nurse**
RSD **Royal Society of Dublin**
RSE **Received Standard English**
RSE **Royal Society of Edinburgh**
RSFSR **Russian Soviet Federal Socialist Republic**, the largest constituent republic of the USSR. In 1991 it became the Russian Federation.
RSG **rate-support grant**
RSGB **Radio Society of Great Britain**
RSH **Royal Society for the Promotion of Health**
RSI **repetitive strain injury**, the inflammation of tendon sheaths in the hands and wrists, caused by repetitive movements such as typing or factory work
RSJ **rolled-steel joist**
RSL **Royal Society of Literature**
RSM **regimental sergeant major**
RSM **Republic of San Marino**, international vehicle registration
RSM **Royal Society of Medicine**
RSM **Royal Society of Musicians of Great Britain**

RSMA **Royal Society of Marine Artists**
RSME **Royal School of Military Engineering**
RSNC **Royal Society for Nature Conservation**
RSNZ **Royal Society of New Zealand**
RSO **Radio Symphony Orchestra**
RSO **Royal Scottish Orchestra**
RSocMed **Royal Society of Medicine**
RSPB **Royal Society for the Protection of Birds**
RSPCA **Royal Society for the Prevention of Cruelty to Animals**
RSPP **Royal Society of Portrait Painters**
RSRE **Royal Signals and Radar Establishment**
RSS **Royal Statistical Society**
RSSA **Royal Scottish Society of Arts**
RSTM & H **Royal Society of Tropical Medicine and Hygiene**
RSV **Revised Standard Version**, of the Bible
RSVP ***répondez s'il vous plaît*** (French), please reply; used on invitations
rte **route**
RTE **Radio Telefis Eireann** (Gaelic), Irish Radio and Television
RTE *(Computing)* **real-time execution**
Rt Hon. **Right Honourable**, the title of British members of parliament
RTITB **Road Transport Industry Training Board**
RTL *(Computing)* **real-time language**
RTL *(Electronics)* **resistor-transistor logic**
RTOL **reduced takeoff and landing**
RTPI **Royal Town Planning Institute**
Rt Rev. **Right Reverend**
RTS **Religious Tract Society**
RTS **Royal Television Society**
RTS **Royal Toxophilite Society**
RTT **radioteletype**
RTU *(Military)* **returned to unit**
RTYC **Royal Thames Yacht Club**
RTZ **Rio Tinto Zinc Corporation**
Ru chemical symbol for **ruthenium**
RU **Republic of Burundi**, international vehicle registration
RU **Rugby Union**
RUC **Royal Ulster Constabulary**

RUG *(Computing)* **restricted users group**
RUI **Royal University of Ireland**
Rukba *or* **RUKBA** **Royal United Kingdom Beneficent Association**
RURAL **Society for the Responsible Use of Resources in Agriculture and on the Land**
RUSI **Royal United Services Institute for Defence Studies**
RV **Det Radicale Venstre**, Radical Liberals, a Danish radical internationalist, left-of-centre political party
RV **recreational vehicle**
RV **Revised Version**, of the Bible
RVC **Royal Veterinary College**
RVCI **Royal Veterinary College of Ireland**
RW **Right Worshipful**
RW **Right Worthy**
RWA **Royal West of England Academy**
RWA **Rwanda**, international vehicle registration
r.w.d **rear-wheel drive**
rwy *or* **Rwy** **railway**
RYA **Royal Yachting Association**

S

s symbol for **second**, a unit of time
S postcode for **Sheffield**
S symbol for **siemens**, a unit of electric conductance
S **small**; used on clothing labels
S **south**
S chemical symbol for **sulphur**
S **Sweden**, international vehicle registration
SA **Salvation Army**
SA **Society of Antiquaries**
SA **Society of Arts**
SA **Society of Authors**
SA **Soil Association**, a pioneer British ecological organization that promotes organic farming
SA **South Africa**
SA **South America**
SA **South Australia**, an Australian state
SA **Sturmabteilung** (German), storm troopers, Nazi terrorist militia
SA postcode for **Swansea**
SAA **small arms ammunition**
SAA **South African Airways**
SAA *(Computing)* **systems application architecture**
Saab *or* **SAAB** **Svensk Aeroplan Aktiebolag**, Swedish aircraft and car company
SAAF **South African Air Force**
SAARC **South Asian Association for Regional Cooperation**
SAB **Society of American Bacteriologists**
SABC **South African Broadcasting Corporation**
Sabena *or* **SABENA** **Société anonyme belge d'exploitation de la navigation aérienne**, Belgian World Airlines
SAC **Senior Aircraftman**

SAC **Strategic Air Command**, the headquarters commanding all US land-based strategic missile and bomber forces, located in Colorado

Saceur *or* **SACEUR** **Supreme Allied Commander Europe**, part of NATO's military command

SACLANT **Supreme Allied Commander Atlantic**, part of NATO's military command

SACSEA **Supreme Allied Command, SE Asia**, part of NATO's military command

SACW **Senior Aircraftwoman**

SAD **seasonal affective disorder**, a recurrent depression characterized by an increased incidence at a particular time of the year

SADCC **Southern African Development Coordination Conference**, an economic organization. The member states are Angola, Botswana, Lesotho, Malawi, Mozambique, Swaziland, Tanzania, Zambia and Zimbabwe.

s.a.e. *or* **SAE** **stamped addressed envelope** *or* **self-addressed envelope**

SAEF **Stock Exchange Automatic Execution Facility**

S Afr. **South Africa**

SAG **Screen Actors' Guild**, a US trade union for television and film actors

SAGB **Spiritualist Association of Great Britain**

SAGE *(Military) (US, Canada)* **semiautomatic ground environment**

SAH **Supreme Allied Headquarters**

SAIDS *(Medicine)* **simian acquired immune deficiency syndrome**

Salop **Shropshire**, an English county

SALT **Strategic Arms Limitation Talks**, a series of US–Soviet discussions (1969–79) aimed at reducing the rate of nuclear arms build-up

Sam. *(Bible)* **Samuel**

S Am. **South America**

SAM **surface-to-air missile**

SAN **styrene-acrylo-nitrile** (a polymer)

S & H **shipping and handling**

S & L **savings and loan association**, the US name for a building society

S & M **sadism and masochism**
Sands *or*
SANDS **Stillbirth and Neonatal Death Society**
S & T **Salmon and Trout Association**
Sane **Schizophrenia -- A National Emergency**
SANROC **South African Non-Racial Olympics Committee**
SAR **search and rescue**
SAR **Sons of the American Revolution**, a society of men descended from patriots of the Revolutionary War
SARAH **search and rescue and homing**
SARCC **South Asia Regional Cooperation Committee**, an organization established in 1983 by India, Pakistan, Bangladesh, Nepal, Sri Lanka, Bhutan, and the Maldives to cover agriculture, telecommunications, health, population, sports, art, and culture
Sarl. **société à responsabilité limitée** (French), private limited company
SARSAT **search and rescue satellite-aided tracking**
SAS **Scandinavian Airlines System**
SAS **Special Air Service**, a specialist British regiment recruited from regiments throughout the army
SASE *(US)* **self-addressed, stamped envelope**
Sask. **Saskatchewan**, a Canadian province
SASO **Senior Air Staff Officer**
SAT *(US)* **scholarship aptitude test**, an examination taken by students wishing to attend US universities
SAT **South Australian Time**
SAT *(Education)* **standard assessment task**
SATB **soprano, alto, tenor, bass**
SATRO **Science and Technology Regional Organization**
S Aus. **South Australia**, an Australian state
SAYE **save as you earn**, a savings scheme
Sb chemical symbol for **antimony**
SB ***Scientiae Baccalaureus*** (Latin), Bachelor of Science, a US degree
SB **Special Branch**
SBA *(Aeronautics)* **standard beam approach**
SBAC **Society of British Aerospace Companies**
SBC **single-board computer**
SBN **standard book number** (replaced by ISBN)

SBP systolic blood pressure
SBR styrene-butadiene rubber
SBS **sick building syndrome**, a malaise found among office workers, caused by pollutants common in air-conditioned buildings
SBS **Special Boat Service**, the Royal Navy's equivalent of the Special Air Service
SBU **strategic business unit**
sc. *scilicet* (Latin), let it be understood
s.c. *(Printing)* **small capitals**
s/c **self-contained**
Sc chemical symbol for **scandium**
SC *(Australia, New Zealand)* **School Certificate**
SC **Security Council**, the most powerful body of the United Nations
SC **Signal Corps**
SC postcode for **South Carolina**, a US state
SC **Special Constable**, a part-time volunteer who supplements local police forces as required
SC **Supreme Court**
SCA *(Medicine)* **sickle-cell anaemia**
SCAO **Senior Civil Affairs Officer**
SCAP **Supreme Command** *(or* **Commander) Allied Powers**
SCAPA **Society for Checking the Abuses of Public Advertising**
s. caps *(Printing)* **small capitals**
SCB **Solicitors Complaints Bureau**
SCBU **special care baby unit**, where premature babies are looked after in a hospital
SCC **Sea Cadet Corps**
SCCL **Scottish Council for Civil Liberties**
SCDC **Schools Curriculum Development Committee**
SCE **Scottish Certificate of Education**
SCF **Save the Children Fund**, a worldwide organization that promotes the rights of children to health care, education, welfare, etc.
SCF **Senior Chaplain to the Forces**
scfh **standard cubic feet per hour**
scfm **standard cubic feet per minute**
SCGB **Ski Club of Great Britain**

Sch. school
SCID **severe combined immune deficiency**, a rare condition in which a baby is born without the body's normal defences against infection
sci-fi **science fiction**
SCLC **Southern Christian Leadership Conference**, a US civil-rights organization founded in 1957 by Martin Luther King
SCM **Student Christian Movement**
SCOBEC **Scottish Business Education Council**
SCONUL **Standing Conference of National and University Libraries**
SCOTEC **Scottish Technical Education Council**
SCOTVEC **Scottish Vocational Education Council**
SCP **single-cell protein**
SCPS **Society of Civil and Public Servants**
SCR **senior common room**, in a university
SCR *(Electronics)* **silicon-controlled rectifier**
SCSI **small computer systems interface**
scuba **self-contained underwater breathing apparatus**
s.d. **semi-detached**
s.d. *(Statistics)* **standard deviation**
SD **semi-detached**
SD *(Medicine)* **senile dementia**
SD **Sicherheitsdienst** (German), the Nazi Security Service
SD **Socialdemokratiet**, Social Democrats, a Danish left-of-centre political party
SD postcode for **South Dakota**, a US state
SD **Swaziland**, international vehicle registration
SDA **Scottish Development Agency**
SDA **Seventh Day Adventists**
S. Dak. **South Dakota**, a US state
SDAT *(Medicine)* **senile dementia of the Alzheimer type**
S-DAT **stationary digital audio tape**
SDC **Society of Dyers and Colourists**
SDD **Scottish Development Department**
SDD *(Telephony)* **subscriber direct dialling**
SDF **Social Democratic Federation**, a socialist society founded in Britain in 1881, becoming the British Socialist Party in 1911

SDI **Strategic Defense Initiative**, the attempt by the US to develop a defence system against incoming nuclear missiles, based in part outside the Earth's atmosphere. It is popularly known as Star Wars.

SDIO *(US)* **Strategic Defense Initiative Office**

SDLP **Social Democratic and Labour Party**, a Northern Irish moderate left-of-centre political party

SDP **Social Democratic Party**, a British centrist political party 1981–90

SDR **special drawing right**, the right of a member state of the International Monetary Fund to apply for money to finance its balance of payments deficit

SDS **sodium dodecyl sulphate** (detergent)

SDT **Society of Dairy Technology**

s.e. *(Statistics)* **standard error**

Se chemical symbol for **selenium**

SE **Society of Engineers**

SE **southeast**

SE postcode for **southeast London**

SEAC **School Examination and Assessment Council**

SEAL **sea, air, land** (team)

SEAQ **Stock Exchange Automated Quotations**, a computerized system of share price monitoring

SEATO **South East Asia Treaty Organization**, a collective defence system 1954–77 established by Australia, France, New Zealand, Pakistan, the Philippines, Thailand, the UK, and the US, with Vietnam, Cambodia, and Laos as protocol states

sec *(Maths)* **secant**

sec **second**

SEC **Securities and Exchange Commission**, the official US agency created to ensure full disclosure to the investing public and protection against malpractice in the securities and financial markets

SECAM ***séquentiel couleur à mémoire*** (French), a colour television broadcasting system

Sec. Gen. **Secretary General**

SED **Scottish Education Department**

SEEB **Southeastern Electricity Board**

SEG **socioeconomic grade**

SELA — **Sistema Económico Latino-Americana**, Latin American Economic System, an international organization for economic, technological, and scientific cooperation in Latin America.

s.e.(m.) *or* **SE(M)** — *(Statistics)* **standard error (of the mean)**

SEM — **scanning electron microscope**

Sen. — **Senator**

SEN — **special educational needs**

SEN — **State Enrolled Nurse**, replaced by Enrolled Nurse (General)

SEO — **Society of Education Officers**

seq. — ***sequentes*** (Latin), the following

seq. luce — ***sequenti luce*** (Latin), the following day; used in prescriptions

SERA — **Socialist Environment and Resources Association**

SERC — **Science and Engineering Research Council**

Serg. — **Sergeant**

Serj. — **Serjeant**

Serps *or* **SERPS** — **State Earnings-Related Pension Scheme**, the British state pension scheme

SERT — **Society of Electronic and Radio Technicians**

SESO — **Senior Equipment Staff Officer**

SETI — *(Astronomy)* **search for extraterrestrial intelligence**

sf — **science fiction**

SF — **Finland**, international vehicle registration

SF — **San Francisco**, a US city

SF — **science fiction**

SF — **Sinn Féin**, an Irish nationalist political party

SF — **Socialistisk Folkeparti**, Socialist People's Party, a Danish moderate left-wing political party

SFA — **Scottish Football Association**

SFC — **specific fuel consumption**

sfm — **surface feet per minute**

SFO — **Serious Fraud Office**

SFT — **supercritical fluid technology**

SFU — **suitable for upgrade**; used on airline tickets

s.g. — **specific gravity**

SG — **Secretary General**

SG **Society of Genealogists**
SG **Solicitor General**
SG postcode for **Stevenage**
SG **Surgeon General**
SGA **Society of Graphic Art**
SGHWR **steam-generating heavy-water reactor**
S. Glam **South Glamorgan**, a Welsh county
SGML *(Computing)* **standard generalized markup language**
SGP **Singapore**, international vehicle registration
Sgt **Sergeant**
SGT **Society of Glass Technology**
Sgt Maj. **Sergeant Major**
s.h. **second-hand**
SHA **Secondary Heads Association**
SHA **Special Health Authority**
SHAEF **Supreme Headquarters Allied Expeditionary Force**, the World War II military centre established on 15 Feb 1944 in London, where final plans were made for the Allied invasion of Europe
SHAPE **Supreme Headquarters Allied Powers Europe**, the headquarters of NATO's Supreme Allied Commander Europe (SACEUR)
SHF *(Physics)* **superhigh frequency**
SHHD **Scottish Home and Health Department**
s/hist **service history**; used in car advertisements
SHM *(Physics)* **simple harmonic motion**, movement such as that of a pendulum, n which the object or point moves so that its acceleration towards a central point is proportional to its distance from it
SHO **Senior House Officer**
shoran **short-range navigation**
shp **shaft horsepower**
Si chemical symbol for **silicon**
SI **South Island**, New Zealand
SI **Staten Island**, an island in New York harbour
SI **styrene isoprene** (a polymer)
SI **Système International (d'Unités)** (French), International System (of Metric Units). SI units are the standard system of scientific units used by scientists worldwide.
SIA **Society of Investment Analysts**

SIA **Spinal Injuries Association**
SIB **Securities and Investment Board**, the British body with overall responsibility for policing financial dealings in the City of London
SIB **self-injurious behaviour**
SIB **Shipbuilding Industry Board**
SIBOR **Singapore InterBank Offered Rate**
SIC **Standard Industrial Classification**
SIDS **sudden infant death syndrome**, commonly known as cot death, the death of an apparently healthy baby in its sleep
SIESO **Society of Industrial and Emergency Service Officers**
Sig. *Signor* (Italian), Mr
Sig. *Signore* (Italian), Sir
SIG **special-interest group**
Sigint *or* **SIGINT** **signals intelligence** (gathering network)
SIM **Société internationale de musicologie** (French), International Musicological Society
SIMA **Scientific Instrument Manufacturers' Association of Great Britain**
SIMA *(Psychiatry)* **system for identifying motivated abilities**
SIMC **Société internationale pour la musique contemporaine** (French), International Society for Contemporary Music
Simca *or* **SIMCA** **Société industrielle de mécanique et carrosserie automobiles**, a French car manufacturer
SIME **Security Intelligence Middle East**
SIMG **Societas Internationalis Medicinae Generalis** (Latin), International Society of General Medicine
SIMM *(Computing, Electronics)* **single in-line memory module**
sin *(Maths)* **sine**
sing. *(Grammar)* **singular**
sinh *(Maths)* **hyperbolic sine**
SINS **ship's inertial navigation system**
SIO *(Computing)* **serial input/output**
SIPC **Securities Investor Protection Corporation**
SIPO *(Computing)* **serial in, parallel out**
SIPRI **Stockholm International Peace Research Institute**
SIS **Secret Intelligence Service**, commonly known as MI6
sit. vac. **situation vacant**

SITA **Société internationale de télécommunications aéronautiques** (French), International Society of Aeronautical Telecommunications
SITC **Standard International Trade Classification**
SITPRO **Simpler Trade Procedures Board**
SIW **self-inflicted wound**
SJ **Society of Jesus**; used after the name of Jesuits
SJ **supersonic jet**
SJA **St John Ambulance**
SJAA **St John Ambulance Association**
SJAB **St John Ambulance Brigade**
SJC *(US)* **Supreme Judicial Court**
SK postcode for **Stockport**
Skr. **Sanskrit**
Skt **Sanskrit**
SL postcode for **Slough**
SLA **Symbionese Liberation Army**
SLADE **Society of Lithographic Artists, Designers, Engravers, and Process Workers**
SLAET **Society of Licensed Aircraft Engineers and Technologists**
Slam *or* **SLAM** **standoff land-attack missile**
Slar *or* **SLAR** **side-looking airborne radar**
SLAS **Society for Latin American Studies**
SLBM **submarine-launched ballistic missile**
SLCM **sea-launched cruise missile**
SLD **self-locking device**
SLD **Social and Liberal Democrats**, the official name for the British centrist political party formed in 1988 from the former Liberal Party and most of the Social Democratic Party. The common name for the party is the Liberal Democrats.
S level **Special level**, an examination which can be taken by 18-year-olds in Britain, usually at the same time as A levels
Slipar **short light pulse alerting receiver** (in an aircraft)
SLP **Scottish Labour Party**
SLR **single-lens reflex**, a type of camera in which the image can be seen through the lens before a picture is taken

s-m *or* **s/m** **sadomasochism** *or* **sadomasochist**
Sm chemical symbol for **samarium**
SM **sadomasochism** *or* **sadomasochist**
SM ***Scientiae Magister*** (Latin), Master of Science, a US degree
SM **Sergeant Major**
SM **Society of Miniaturists**
SM **Staff Major**
SM postcode for **Sutton**
SMATV **satellite master antenna television**
SMBG *(Medicine)* **self-monitoring of blood glucose**
sm. caps *(Printing)* **small capitals**
SMD *(Medicine)* **senile macular degeneration**
SME **Suriname**, international vehicle registration
Smersh *or* **SMERSH** **Smert Shpionam** (Russian), death to spies, a section of the KGB
SMLE **short magazine Lee-Enfield** (rifle)
SMMT **Society of Motor Manufacturers and Traders Ltd**
SMO **Senior Medical Officer**
SMON *(Medicine)* **sub-acute myelo-opticoneuropathy**
SMP **statutory maternity pay**
SMR **standard Malaysian rubber**
SMR **standard metabolic rate**
SMSA **Standard Metropolitan Statistical Area**, a US city area chosen for gathering demographic data
Sn chemical symbol for **tin**
SN **Senegal**, international vehicle registration
SN postcode for **Swindon**
SNA *(Computing)* **systems network architecture**
SNAP **systems for nuclear auxiliary power**
SNCB **Société nationale des chemins de fer belges** (French), Belgian National Railways
SNCC *(US)* **Student Nonviolent** (*or* **National**) **Coordinating Committee**
SNCF **Société nationale des chemins de fers français** (French), state railway authority
SNG **substitute** (*or* **synthetic**) **natural gas**
SNH **Scottish National Heritage**
SNIG **sustainable non-inflationary growth**

SNO	**Senior Naval Officer**
SNP	**Scottish National Party**, a Scottish nationalistic political party
Snr	**Senior**
SNR	**Society for Nautical Research**
SNR	*(Astronomy)* **supernova remnant**
SNTS	**Society for New Testament Studies**
SNU	*(Astronomy)* **solar neutrino unit**
s.o.	*(Baseball)* **strikeout**
SO	**Scientific Officer**
SO	**Signal Officer**
SO	postcode for **Southampton**
SO	**Staff Officer**
SO	**Stationery Office**
SO	**Symphony Orchestra**
SOA	**state of the art**
SOAP	**subjective, objective, analysis, plan**, a method used for compiling medical records
Soc.	**Socialist**
Soc.	**Society**
SOCO	**scene-of-crime officer**
SOCS	**Society of County Secretaries**
SODAC	**Society of Dyers and Colourists**
SODEPAX	**Committee on Society, Development, and Peace**
SOE	**Special Operations Executive**, in World War II
SOE	**state-owned enterprise**
S. of S.	**Secretary of State**
soh	**sense of humour**; used in newspaper lonely hearts advertisements
Sol.	*(Bible)* **Song of Solomon**
Solace *or* **SOLACE**	**Society of Local Authority Chief Executives**
Sol. Gen.	**Solicitor General**
Som	**Somerset**, an English county
SOM	**Society of Occupational Medicine**
sonar	**sound navigation and ranging**, a method of locating underwater objects by the reflection of ultrasonic waves
Song	*(Bible)* **Song of Solomon**
SOP	**standard operating procedure**
SOP	*(Computing)* **sum of products**

SoR *or* **SOR** **sale or return**
s.o.s. ***si opus sit*** (Latin), if necessary; used in prescriptions
SOS **save our souls**, an internationally recognized distress signal in Morse code (...- - -...)
SoS *or* **SOS** **Secretary of State**
SOSc **Society of Ordained Scientists**
SOTS **Society for Old Testament Study**
Soweto **South West Township**, a racially segregated urban settlement in South Africa
s.p. *or* **SP** **starting price**; used in horse racing
SP **postcode for Salisbury**
SP **Self-Propelled** (Antitank Regiment)
SP **submarine patrol**
SpA ***società per azioni*** (Italian), public limited company
SPAB **Society for the Protection of Ancient Buildings**
SPARC *(Computing)* **scalable processor architecture**
SPC **Southern Pacific Commission**, an economic organization of countries in the region
SPC *(Telephony)* **stored-program control**
SPCA *(US)* **Society for the Prevention of Cruelty to Animals**
SPCC *(US)* **Society for the Prevention of Cruelty to Children**
SPCK **Society for Promoting Christian Knowledge**
SPD **Sozialdemokratische Partei Deutschlands**, Social Democratic Party of Germany, a left-of-centre political party
SPE **Society of Pure English**
SPEC **South Pacific Bureau for Economic Cooperation**, an organization founded for the purpose of stimulating economic cooperation and the development of trade in the region
SPECT *(Medicine)* **single photon emission computed tomography**
SPF **South Pacific Forum**, an association of states in the region that discusses common interests and develops common policies
SPF **sun protection factor**, a number showing the degree of protection from the sun given by a sunscreen product
SPG **Special Patrol Group**, a squad of experienced police officers concentrating on a specific problem
SPGB **Socialist Party of Great Britain**

sp. gr. **specific gravity**
sp. ht **specific heat**
SPLA **Sudan People's Liberation Army**
SPMO **Senior Principal Medical Officer**
SPNM **Society for the Promotion of New Music**
SPOD **Sexual Problems of the Disabled**, a department of the Royal Association for Disability and Rehabilitation
SPQR **Senatus Populusque Romanus** (Latin), the Senate and the Roman People
Spr **Sapper**
SPR **Society for Psychical Research**
SPRC **Society for the Prevention and Relief of Cancer**
SPREd **Society of Picture Researchers and Editors**
SPRL **Society for the Promotion of Religion and Learning**
SPS **syndiotactic polystyrene** (a plastic)
SPSO **Senior Principal Scientific Officer**
SPTL **Society of Public Teachers of Law**
Spuc *or* **SPUC** **Society for the Protection of the Unborn Child**
SPURV **self-propelled underwater research vehicle**
Sq. **Square**; used in street names
SQ **sick quarters**
SQ **stereophonic-quadrophonic**
SQA *(Computing)* **software quality assurance**
sq cm **square centimetre**
Sqdn Ldr **Squadron Leader**
sq ft **square foot**
sq in **square inch**
sq km **square kilometre**
SQL *(Computing)* **standard query language**
SQL *(Computing)* **structured query language**, designed for use with relational databases
sq m **square metre**
sq mi **square mile**
sq mm **square millimetre**
Sqn Ldr **Squadron Leader**
sq yd **square yard**
sr symbol for **steradian**, unit of measurement for solid angles
Sr *Senhor* (Portuguese), Mr *or* Sir
Sr **Senior**; used after a name

Sr *Señor* (Spanish), Mr or Sir
Sr chemical symbol for **strontium**
SR **Society of Radiographers**
SR *(US)* **Sons of the Revolution**
SR *(Military)* **Special Reserve**
SR postcode for **Sunderland**
S/R **sale or return**
Sra *Senhora* (Portuguese), Mrs
Sra *Señora* (Spanish), Mrs
SRA **Squash Rackets Association**
SRAM **short-range attack missile**
SRAM *(Computing)* **static random-access memory**, a memory device in the form of a silicon chip
SR & CC **strikes, riot, and civil commotion**
SRBM **short-range ballistic missile**
SRC **Students' Representative Council**
SRCh **State Registered Chiropodist**
SRG **Strategic Research Group**
SRHE **Society for Research into Higher Education**
SRI **Sacrum Romanum Imperium** (Latin), Holy Roman Empire
SRIS **Science Reference Information Service**
SRN **State Registered Nurse**, former name for RGN, Registered General Nurse
sRNA **soluble RNA**
SRNA **Shipbuilders and Repairers National Association**
SRO **self-regulatory organization**
SRO **single-room occupancy** (in a hotel)
SRO **standing room only**
SRO **Statutory Rules and Orders**
SRO **Supplementary Reserve of Officers**
s/roof **sunroof**; used in car advertisements
SRP **State Registered Physiotherapist**
SRP **suggested retail price**
Srta *Senhorita* (Portuguese), Miss
Srta *Señorita* (Spanish), Miss
SRU **Scottish Rugby Union**
SS **Saints**
SS **Schutzstaffel** (German), protection squadron, the Nazi elite corps

SS	**Secretary of State**
SS	**secret service**
SS	postcode for **Southend-on-Sea**
SS	**steamship**; used in the names of US ships
SSA	**Society of Scottish Artists**
SSA	**standard spending assessment**
SSAC	**Social Security Advisory Committee**
SSAE	**stamped self-addressed envelope**
SSAFA	**Soldiers', Sailors', and Airmen's Families Association**
SSAP	**Statement of Standard Accounting Practice**
SSBN	*(US)* **strategic submarine, ballistic nuclear**
SSC	**Scottish Ski Club**
SSC	**Short Service Commission**
SSC	**Species Survival Commission**
SSD	**Social Services Department**
SS.D	***Sanctissimus Dominus*** (Latin), Most Holy Lord, the Pope
SSE	**south-southeast**
SSEB	**South of Scotland Electricity Board**
SEES	**School of Slavonic and East European Studies**, at the University of London
SSF	**single-seater fighter** (aircraft)
S/Sgt	**Staff Sergeant**
SSI	**Social Services Inspectorate**
SSI	**Society of Scribes and Illuminators**
SSI	*(US)* **Supplemental Security Income**, for the aged, blind, and disabled
SSM	**surface-to-surface missile**
SSN	**severely subnormal**
SSN	*(US)* **Social Security Number**
SSN	**Standard Serial Number**
SSO	**Senior Scientific Officer**
SSO	**Senior Supply Officer**
SSP	**statutory sick pay**
SSPCA	**Scottish Society for the Prevention of Cruelty to Animals**
SSPE	*(Medicine)* **subacute sclerosing panencephalitis**
SSR	**secondary surveillance radar**
SSR	**Soviet Socialist Republic**
SSS	*(Golf)* **standard scratch score**

SSSI **site of special scientific interest**, land that has been identified as having animals, plants, or geological features that need to be protected and conserved
SST **Society of Surveying Technicians**
SST **supersonic transport**
SSTA **Scottish Secondary Teachers' Association**
SSW **south-southwest**
st. *(Printing)* **stet**
st. **stone**
st. *(Cricket)* **stumped**
s.t. **short ton**
St **Saint**
St. **Strait**
St. **Street**
ST **Space Telescope** (the Hubble telescope)
ST **Standard Time**
ST postcode for **Stoke-on-Trent**
ST **Summer Time**
Sta. **Station**
STA **Sail Training Association**
Staffs **Staffordshire**, an English county
STAGS **Sterling Transferable Accruing Government Securities**
START **Strategic Arms Reduction Talks**, a phase in US–Soviet peace discussions, beginning with talks in Geneva in 1983
stat. ***statim*** (Latin), immediately; used in prescriptions
stbd **starboard**
STC **Senior Training Corps**
STC **Short-Title Catalogue**
STD **sexually transmitted disease**
STD *(New Zealand)* **subscriber toll dialling**
STD **subscriber trunk dialling**, a British system allowing people to connect their own long-distance telephone calls by use of a special number (the STD code) for each telephone exchange
Sté ***société*** (French), company
STE **Society of Telecom Executives**, a British trade union
STEM **scanning transmission electron microscope**
Sten a gun named after its inventors, **Shepherd and Turpin of Enfield**
STEP **Special Temporary Employment Programme**

STIM	**scanning transmission ion microscope**
STM	**scanning tunnelling microscope**, a microscope that produces a magnified image by moving a tiny tungsten probe across the surface of the specimen
STM	**short-term memory**
STOL	**short takeoff and landing**, aircraft fitted with special devices on the wings that increase aerodynamic lift at low speeds
STOVL	**short takeoff and vertical landing**
stp	**standard temperature and pressure**, a standard set of conditions for experimental measurements
STP	**scientifically treated petroleum**, colloquial name of an hallucinogenic drug
STP	**standard temperature and pressure**, a standard set of conditions for experimental measurements
STRIVE	**Society for the Preservation of Rural Industries and Village Enterprises**
STSO	**Senior Technical Staff Officer**
STUC	**Scottish Trades Union Congress**
STV	**Scottish Television**
STV	**single transferable vote**
SU	**Scripture Union**
subj.	**subject**
subj.	*(Grammar)* **subjunctive**
Sub-Lieut.	**Sub-Lieutenant**
Sub-Lt	**Sub-lieutenant**
suff.	**suffix**
Suff	**Suffolk**, an English county
SUM	**surface-to-underwater missile**
SUNY	**State University of New York**
Sup. Ct	**Superior Court**
Sup. Ct	**Supreme Court**
superl.	**superlative**
Supp. Res.	**Supplementary Reserve** (of Officers)
Supt	**Superintendent**
Surr	**Surrey**, an English county
Surv. Gen.	**Surveyor General**
SUT	**Society for Underwater Technology**
Sv	symbol for **sievert**, a unit of radiation dose equivalent
SV	**stroke volume** (of an engine)

SVD **swine vesicular disease**
SVGA *(Computing)* **super video graphics array**
S-VHS **super-VHS**
SVS **still-camera video system**
SW **short wave**
SW **southwest**
SW postcode for **southwest London**
S/W *(Computing)* **software**
SWA **Namibia**, international vehicle registration
SWAPO **South West Africa People's Organization**, a Namibian political party founded in 1959 to oppose South African rule
SWAT **Special Weapons and Tactics**, a US police unit
SWCI *(Computing)* **software configuration item**
SWEB **South Wales Electricity Board**
SWEB **Southwest Electricity Board**
SWET **Society of West End Theatre**
SWG **standard wire gauge**
SWIE **South Wales Institute of Engineers**
SWIFT **Society for Worldwide Interbank Financial Transmission**
Swing *(Finance)* **Sterling warrant into gilt-edged stock**
SWLA **Society of Wildlife Artists**
SWOT **strengths, weaknesses, opportunities, threats**, a way of analysing a company or product's place in the market vis-à-vis its competitors
SWPA **South West Pacific Area**
SWR *(Telecommunications)* **standing-wave radio**
SY **Seychelles**, international vehicle registration
SY postcode for **Shrewsbury**
SYHA **Scottish Youth Hostels Association**
S. Yorks **South Yorkshire**, an English county
SYR **Syria**, international vehicle registration

T

t	**ton** *or* **tonne**
t.	**teaspoon(ful)**
T	symbol for **tesla**, a unit of magnetic flux density
T	**Thailand**, international vehicle registration
T	**telephone**; used on maps
T.	**tablespoon(ful)**
Ta	chemical symbol for **tantalum**
TA	postcode for **Taunton**
TA	**Territorial Army**
TA	**Translators Association**
TAA	**Territorial Army Association**
TAA	**Trans-Australia Airlines**
TA & VRA	**Territorial Auxiliary and Volunteer Reserve Association**
TAB	**tabulator**; used on a keyboard
TAB	*(Australia, New Zealand)* **Totalizator Administration** (*or* **Agency**) **Board**
TAB	**typhoid, paratyphoid A, paratyphoid B** (vaccine)
TABM	**tactical antiballistic missile**
TAC	**Tactical Air Command**
TACAN	**tactical air navigation**
TACV	**tracked air-cushion vehicle**
TADA	**taking and driving away** (an offence)
Tads	*(Military)* **target acquisition and designation sight**
TAF	**Tactical Air Force**
TAFE	**technical and further education**
Talisman *or* **TALISMAN**	**Transfer Accounting Lodgement for Investors and Stock Management**
TAM	**Television Audience Measurement**
Tamba	**Twins and Multiple Births Association**
tan	*(Maths)* **tangent**
tanh	*(Maths)* **hyperbolic tan**

T & AFA	**Territorial and Auxiliary Forces Association**
T & AVR	**Territorial and Army Volunteer Reserve**
T & E	**travel and entertainment**
T & E	**trial and error**
t & g.	**tongued and grooved** (wood)
T & G	**Transport and General Workers' Union**, a British trade union
t. & s.	**toilet and shower**
T & T	**taxed and tested**; used in car advertisements
TANU	**Tanganyika African National Union**, a moderate socialist national party of the 1950s and 60s
TAP	**Transportes Aéreos Portugueses**, Portuguese Airlines
TAPS	**Trans-Alaska Pipeline System**
TARO	**Territorial Army Reserve of Officers**
TAS	*(Aeronautics)* **true air speed**
TASI	*(Telecommunications)* **time-assignment speech interpolation**
TASM	**tactical air-to-surface missile**
Tass	**Telegrafnoye Agentstvo Sovyetskovo Soyuza** (Russian), the Soviet news agency
TAT	*(Psychology)* **thematic apperception test**
TAT	*(Medicine)* **tired all the time**
TAURUS	**Transfer and Automated Registration of Uncertified Stock**
TAVR	**Territorial and Army Volunteer Reserve**
TAVR	**Territorial Auxiliary and Volunteer Reserve Association**
Tb	chemical symbol for **terbium**
TB	**torpedo boat**
TB	**Treasury bill**
TB	**tuberculosis**
t.b.a.	**to be advised**
t.b.a.	**to be agreed**
t.b.a.	**to be announced**
TBD	**torpedo-boat destroyer**
TBF	**Teachers Benevolent Fund**
TBI	**throttle-body injection**
TBI	**total body irradiation**
TBM	**tactical ballistic missile**
TBO	*(Aeronautics)* **time between overhauls**

tbs.	**tablespoon(ful)**
TBT	**tributyl tin**, a chemical used in antifouling paint
Tc	chemical symbol for **technetium**
TCA	**tricarboxylic acid**
TCA	**trichloroacetic acid** (a herbicide)
TCA	**tricyclic antidepressant** (a drug)
TCB	**tetrachlorobiphenyl**
TCBM	**transcontinental ballistic missile**
TCCB	**Test and County Cricket Board**
TCDD	**tetrachlorodibenzodioxin** (an environmental pollutant)
TCE	**trichloroethylene** (a solvent)
tcf	**trillion cubic feet**
TCF	**Touring Club de France**
TCP	*(Computing)* **transmission control protocol**
TCP	(trademark) **trichlorophenylmethyliodisalicyl** (an antiseptic)
TCPA	**Town and Country Planning Association**
TD	postcode for **Galashiels**
TD	*(Medicine)* **tardive dyskinesia**
TD	***Teachta Dála*** (Gaelic), Member of the **Dáil**, the Irish parliament
TD	*(American football)* **touchdown**
TDL	**tunable diode laser**
TDMA	*(Telecommunications)* **time-division multiple access**
TDN	**total digestible nutrients**
TDRS *or* **TDRSS**	**tracking and data-relay satellite system**
t.d.s.	***ter die sumendum*** (Latin), to be taken three times a day; used in prescriptions
TDS	*(Computing)* **tabular data stream**
t/e	**twin-engined**
Te	chemical symbol for **tellurium**
TEAC	**Technical Educational Advisory Council**
TEC	**Training and Enterprise Council**
TEE	**Trans-Europe Express**
TEF	**toxicity equivalence factor**
TEFL	**teaching of English as a foreign language**
tel.	**telephone**
TEL	**tetraethyl lead** (a petrol additive)
telecom.	**telecommunications**

telex **teleprinter exchange** *or* **teletypewriter exchange**
tel. no. **telephone number**
TEMA **Telecommunications Engineering and Manufacturing Association**
temp. **temperature**
temp. **temporary**
Templar **tactical expert mission-planner**, a military computer
Tenn. **Tennessee**, a US state
TENS **transcutaneous electrical nerve stimulation**, used as a device for controlling pain, for example in labour
TEPP **tetraethyl pyrophosphate** (a pesticide)
TERCOM **terrain-contour matching**, used by smart weapons to guide the missile to its target
TES **Times Educational Supplement**
TESL **teaching of English as a second language**
TESOL **teaching of English to speakers of other languages**
Tessa *or* **TESSA** **tax-exempt special savings account**, a British scheme to encourage longer-term savings by making interest tax-free on deposits of up to £9,000 over five years
Tewt *or* **TEWT** *(Military)* **tactical exercise without troops**
Tex. **Texas**, a US state
TF postcode for **Telford**
TF **Territorial Force**
TFAP **Tropical Forestry Action Plan**
TFD *(Electronics)* **thin-film detector**
TFR **Territorial Force Reserve**
TFSC **Turkish Federated State of Cyprus**
TFW **tactical fighter wing**
TFX **tactical fighter experimental** (aircraft)
tg *(Maths)* **tangent**
TG **Togo**, international vehicle registration
TGAT *(Education)* **Task Group on Assessment and Testing**
T-gate *(Computing)* **ternary selector gate**
TGEW **Timber Growers England and Wales Ltd**
TGF *(Medicine)* **transforming growth factor**
TGI **Target Group Index**; used in marketing
T-group **training group**
TGV ***train à grande vitesse*** (French), high-speed passenger train

TGWU	**Transport and General Workers' Union**, a British trade union
Th	chemical symbol for **thorium**
THC	**tetrahydrocannabinol** (an ingredient of cannabis)
THD	**total harmonic distortion**
THELEP	**Therapy of Leprosy**
THES	**Times Higher Educational Supplement**
Thess.	*(Bible)* **Thessalonians**
THF	**Trusthouse Forte plc**
THI	**temperature-humidity index**
THORP	**Thermal Oxide Reprocessing Plant**, a plant at Sellafield in Cumbria used for reprocessing uranium and plutonium
thou.	**thousand**
THR	*(Medicine)* **total hip replacement**
thru	**through**
THz	**terahertz**
Ti	chemical symbol for **titanium**
TI	**thermal imaging**
TIA	*(Medicine)* **transient ischaemic attack**
TIBOR	**Tokyo InterBank Offered Rate**
t.i.d.	***ter in die*** (Latin), three times a day; used in prescriptions
TIG	**tungsten inert gas**
TIGR	**Treasury Investment Growth Receipts**
TIH	**Their Imperial Highnesses**
Tim.	*(Bible)* **Timothy**
TIM	**transient intermodulation distortion**
TIMS	**The Institute of Management Sciences**
tinct.	**tincture**
TIP	*(Computing)* **terminal interface processor**
TIR	**Transports Internationaux Routiers** (French), International Road Transport
Tit.	*(Bible)* **Titus**
TJ	**triple jump**
t.k.o. *or* **TKO**	*(Boxing)* **technical knockout**
Tl	chemical symbol for **thallium**
TL	**thermoluminescent**
tlc *or* **TLC**	**tender loving care**
TLC	**total lung capacity**
TLC	*(Australia)* **Trades and Labour Council**

TLG **Theatrical Ladies' Guild**
TLR **twin-lens reflex**, a camera that has a viewing lens of the same angle of view and focal length mounted above and parallel to the taking lens
TLS **Times Literary Supplement**
t.m. *(Statistics)* **true mean**
Tm chemical symbol for **thulium**
TM **trademark**
TM **transcendental meditation**
TM **trench mortar**
TMA **Theatrical Management Association**
TMA **Trans-Mediterranean Airways**, the national airline of Lebanon
TMA **trimellitic acid**
T-man a special investigator of the US Treasury Department (informal term)
TMD *(Military)* **theatre missile defence**
TMJ *(Medicine)* **temporomandibular joint**
TMMG **Teacher of Massage and Medical Gymnastics**
TMO **telegraph money order**
tn **ton** *or* **tonne**
TN postcode for **Tennessee**, a US state
TN postcode for **Tonbridge**
TN **Tunisia**, international vehicle registration
TNC **Theatres National Committee**
TNC **transnational corporation**
TNF *(Military)* **theatre nuclear forces**
TNF *(Medicine)* **tumour necrosis factor**
T-note *(US)* **Treasury note**
tnpk. **turnpike**
TNT **trinitrotoluene**, a powerful high explosive
t.o. **turn over**
TO **Transport Officer**
TO **turn over**
TOE *(Physics)* **theory of everything**, another name for grand unified theory
TOEFL **testing of English as a foreign language**
TOFC **trailer on flat car**
tonn. **tonnage**
t.o.o. **time of origin**

t.o.o. **to order only**
TOO **time of origin**
TOO **to order only**
TOP *(Computing)* **technical office protocol**
TOP **temporarily out of print**
TOPIC **Teletext Output Price Information Computer**
TOPS **Training Opportunities Scheme**
Toshiba **Tokyo Shibaura Denki KK**, a Japanese corporation
TOTC *(Military)* **time-on-target computation**
TOW **tube-launched optically tracked wire-guided** (antitank missile)
TP **teaching practice**
TP **Transvaal Province**, a South African province
TP **trigonometric point**
tPA *or* **TPA** *(Medicine)* **tissue plasminogen activator**, a naturally occurring substance in the body tissues that activates the enzyme plasmin, which is able to dissolve blood clots
TPC *(Australia)* **Trade Practices Commission**
tpd *or* **TPD** **tons per day**
tph *or* **TPH** **tons per hour**
tpi *(Engineering)* **teeth per inch**
tpi *(Computing)* **tracks per inch**
tpi *(Engineering)* **turns per inch**
TPI *(Engineering)* **threads per inch**
TPI **Tropical Products Institute**
tpk. **turnpike**
tpm *or* **TPM** **tons per minute**
TPN *(Medicine)* **total parenteral nutrition**
Tpr **Trooper**
TPR **temperature, pulse, respiration**
TQ postcode for **Torquay**
TQ **total quality**
TQM **total quality management**
TR *(Telecommunications)* **transmit-receive**
TR postcode for **Truro**
TR **Turkey**, international vehicle registration
TRACE *(Aeronautics)* **test equipment for rapid automatic checkout evaluation**
trad. **traditional**
TRC **Thames Rowing Club**

TRDA **Timber Research and Development Association**
TRF **tuned radio frequency**
TRH **Their Royal Highnesses**
TRIC **Television and Radio Industries Club**
trig. **trigonometric** *or* **trigonometry**
TRJ **turboramjet** (engine)
TRM **trademark**
tRNA **transfer RNA**
Trp **tryptophan**
TRRL **Transport and Road Research Laboratory**
TS postcode for **Cleveland**
TS **Treasury Solicitor**
TSA **The Securities Association Ltd**
TSB **Trustee Savings Bank**
TSE **Tokyo Stock Exchange**
TSE *(Medicine)* **transmissible spongiform encephalopathy**
T. Sgt **Technical Sergeant**
TSH **Their Serene Highnesses**
TSH *(Medicine)* **thyroid-stimulating hormone**
tsi **tons per square inch**
TSO **Trading Standards Officer**
TSS **toxic shock syndrome**, a rare condition that can lead to death, caused by a toxin that can accumulate if a tampon is left in the body for longer than four to six hours
tsp. **teaspoon(ful)**
TSR **(Computing) terminate and stay resident**
TSSA **Transport Salaried Staffs' Association**
TSW **Television South West**, a British television company
TT **teetotal**
TT **telegraphic transfer**
TT **Tourist Trophy** (motorcycling races)
TT **Trinidad and Tobago**, international vehicle registration
TT **Trust Territories**, territories formerly held under the United Nations trusteeship system to be prepared for independence
TT **tuberculin-tested**
TTB **tetragonal tungsten bronze**
TTBT **Threshold Test Ban Treaty**
TTC **technical training centre**
TTF **Timber Trade Federation**

TTL **transistor-transistor logic**, a family of integrated circuits with fast switching speeds commonly used in building electronic devices

TU **toxic unit**

TU **trade union**

TUC **Trades Union Congress**, a voluntary organization of British trade unions

TUG **Telephone Users' Group**

TV **television**

TVA **Tennessee Valley Authority**

TVEI **Technical and Vocational Education Initiative**, a scheme intended to expand pre-vocational education in British schools

Tvl **Transvaal**, a South African province

TVP **textured vegetable protein**, a meat substitute usually made from soya beans

TVRO **television receive only** (antenna)

TW *(Telecommunications)* **travelling wave**

TW postcode for **Twickenham**

TWA **Thames Water Authority**

TWA **Trans-World Airlines**, a US airline

TWh **terawatt hour**

TX postcode for **Texas**, a US state

typo **typographical error**

U

U	**universal**, a film classification
U	**upper class**
U	chemical symbol for **uranium**
UA	**United Artists**, a film production company
UAB	**Unemployment Assistance Board**
UAE	**United Arab Emirates**
UAM	**underwater-to-air missile**
u. & l.c.	*(Printing)* **upper and lower case**
UAR	**United Arab Republic**
UARS	**upper-atmosphere research satellite**
UART	**universal asynchronous receiver/transmitter**
UAU	**Universities Athletics Union**
UAW	*(US)* **United Automobile Workers**
UB	postcode for **Southall**
UB40	**Unemployment Benefit 40** (index card)
UBI	**Understanding British Industry**
U-boat	***Unterseeboot*** (German), German submarine
UBR	**Uniform Business Rate** (of taxation)
u.c.	*(Printing)* **upper case**
UCAS	**Universities and Colleges Admissions Service** (formerly Universities Central Council on Admissions), organization dealing with applicants to British universities and colleges
Ucatt *or* UCATT	**Union of Construction, Allied Trades, and Technicians**
UCBSA	**United Cricket Board of South Africa**
Ucca *or* UCCA	**Universities Central Council on Admissions**, former name for the Universities and Colleges Admissions Service
UCET	**Universities Council for Education of Teachers**
UCH	**University College Hospital**, in London
UCITS	**Undertakings for Collective Investment in Transferable Securities**
UCNS	**Universities' Council for Nonacademic Staff**

UCR **unconditioned reflex** *or* **unconditioned response**
UCS **unconditioned stimulus**
UCTA **United Commercial Travellers' Association**
UCW **Union of Communication Workers**
u.d. ***ut dictum*** (Latin), as directed; used in prescriptions
UDA **Ulster Defence Association**
UDC **Urban Development Corporation**
UDC **Urban District Council**
UDF **Ulster Defence Force**
UDF *(South Africa)* **Union Defence Force**
UDF **Union pour la Démocratie Française**, Union for French Democracy, a French centre-right political party
UDF **United Democratic Front**, a South African moderate multiracial political organization
UDI **unilateral declaration of independence**, the declaration of Ian Smith's Rhodesian Front government on 11 Nov 1965, announcing the independence of Rhodesia (now Zimbabwe) from Britain
UDM **Union of Democratic Mineworkers**, a British trade union
UDR **Ulster Defence Regiment**
UE *(New Zealand)* **university entrance** (examination)
UEA **University of East Anglia**
UEFA **Union of European Football Associations**
UF **United Free** (Church, of Scotland)
UF **urea-formaldehyde**
UFAW **Universities Federation for Animal Welfare**
UFC **United Free Church** (of Scotland)
UFC **University Funding Council**
UFF **Ulster Freedom Fighters**
UFO **unidentified flying object**
UFT **unified field theory**
UHF **ultra high frequency**, referring to radio waves of very short wavelength, e.g. for television broadcasting
UHT **ultra heat treated** (milk)
UHT **ultrahigh temperature**
UHV **ultrahigh vacuum**
u/i **under instruction**
UIL **United Irish League**
UIT **unit investment trust**
UK **United Kingdom**

UKA **United Kingdom Alliance**
UKAC **United Kingdom Automation Council**
UKADGE **United Kingdom Air Defence Ground Environment**
UKAEA **United Kingdom Atomic Energy Authority**, a national authority responsible for research and development of all nonmilitary aspects of nuclear energy
UKAPE **United Kingdom Association of Professional Engineers**
UKCC **United Kingdom Central Council for Nursing, Midwifery, and Health Visiting**
UKCIS **United Kingdom Chemical Information Service**
UKCOSA **United Kingdom Council for Overseas Students' Affairs**
UKCSBS **United Kingdom Civil Service Benefit Society**
UKDA **United Kingdom Dairy Association**
UKFBPW **United Kingdom Federation of Business and Professional Women**
UKgal **UK gallon**
Ukias *or* **UKIAS** **United Kingdom Immigrants' Advisory Service**
UKISC **United Kingdom Industrial Space Committee**
UKLF **United Kingdom Land Forces**
UKMF(L) **United Kingdom Military Forces (Land)**
UKMIS **United Kingdom Mission**
UKOOA **United Kingdom Offshore Operators Association**
UKPIA **United Kingdom Petroleum Industry Association Ltd**
UKSLS **United Kingdom Services Liaison Staff**
UKSMA **United Kingdom Sugar Merchant Association Ltd**
ULA **uncommitted logic array**, a type of integrated circuit
ULCC **ultralarge crude carrier** (oil tanker)
ULF **ultralow frequency**
ULMS **underwater long-range missile system**
ULSEB **University of London School Examinations Board**
ULT **United Lodge of Theosophists**
ULV **ultralow volume**
UMB *(Computing)* **upper memory block**
UMDS **United Medical and Dental Schools**
Umist *or* **UMIST** **University of Manchester Institute of Science and Technology**
UMT *(US)* **universal military training**
UMW *(US)* **United Mine Workers**

UN **United Nations**, an association of states for international peace, security, and cooperation

UNA **United Nations Association**

UNBRO **United Nations Border Relief Operation**

UNC **United Nations Command**

UNCAST **United Nations Conference on the Applications of Science and Technology**

UNCDF **United Nations Capital Development Fund**

UNCED **United Nations Conference on Environment and Development**

UNCHS **United Nations Centre for Human Settlements**, a UN agency

UNCIO **United Nations Conference on International Organization**

UNCITRAL **United Nations Commission on International Trade Law**

UNCLOS **United Nations Conference on the Law of the Sea**

UNCSTD **United Nations Conference on Science and Technology for Development**

Unctad *or* **UNCTAD** **United Nations Commission on Trade and Development**, a UN agency

UNDP **United Nations Development Programme**, a UN body that promotes development in developing countries

UNDRO **United Nations Disaster Relief Organization**, a UN agency

Une chemical symbol for **unnilenium**

UNECA **United Nations Economic Commission for Asia**

UNEF **United Nations Emergency Force**

UNEP **United Nations Environmental Programme**, a UN body that promotes cooperation on environmental issues

UNESCO **United Nations Educational, Scientific, and Cultural Organization**, a UN agency

UNFAO **United Nations Food and Agriculture Organization**

UNFICYP **United Nations** (Peace-Keeping) **Force in Cyprus**

UNFPA **United Nations Fund for Population Activities**, a UN agency

Unh chemical symbol for **unnihexium**

UNHCR **United Nations High Commission for Refugees**, a UN agency

UNIA *(US)* **Universal Negro Improvement Association**
Unicef *or* **UNICEF** **United Nations Children's Fund**, a UN agency
UNIDO **United Nations Industrial Development Organization**
Unifil *or* **UNIFIL** **United Nations Interim Force in Lebanon**
Unisist *or* **UNISIST** **Universal System for Information in Science and Technology**
Unit. **Unitarian** *or* **Unitarianism**
UNITA **União Nacional para a Independéncia Total de Angola** (Portuguese), National Union for the Total Independence of Angola, the Angolan nationalist movement backed by South Africa
UNITAR **United Nations Institute for Training and Research**, a UN agency
Univ. **University**
UNIVAC **universal automatic computer**
Uno chemical symbol for **unniloctium**
UNO **United Nations Organization**
Unp chemical symbol for **unnipentium**
UNPO **Unrepresented Nations' and Peoples' Organization**, an association that represents ethnic and minority groups unrecognized by the United Nations, and defends the rights to self-determination of oppressed peoples
UNPROFOR **United Nations Protection Force**
Unq chemical symbol for **unnilquadium**
Unref *or* **UNREF** **United Nations Refugee Emergency Fund**
UNRISD **United Nations Research Institute for Social Development**, a UN agency
Unrra *or* **UNRRA** **United Nations Relief and Rehabilitation Administration**
Uns chemical symbol for **unnilseptium**
UNSCOB **United Nations Special Committee on the Balkans**
UNSCOP **United Nations Special Committee on Palestine**
Untac *or* **UNTAC** **United Nations Transitional Authority for Cambodia**

UP	**United Presbyterian**
UP	**United Press** (news agency)
UPC	**United Presbyterian Church**
UPC	**universal product code**, a bar code used in the US
UPI	**United Press International**, a wire news service based in Washington DC
UPNI	**Unionist Party of Northern Ireland**
UPS	**uninterruptible power supply**
UPS	**United Parcel Service**
UPU	**Universal Postal Union**, a United Nations agency
UPUP	**Ulster Popular Unionist Party**, a Northern Ireland militant right-of-centre political party
uPVC	**unplasticized polyvinyl chloride**
UR	**unconditioned reflex** *or* **unconditioned response**
URC	**United Reformed Church**
URI	**upper respiratory infection**
URTI	**upper respiratory tract infection**
URTU	**United Road Transport Union**
Us	**ultrasound scanning** *or* **ultrasonic scanning**
US	**Undersecretary**
US	**United States**
US	**United States highway, e.g. the US5**
USA	**United States Army**
USA	**United States of America**
USA	**United States of America**, international vehicle registration
USAF	**United States Air Force**
USAID	**United States Agency for International Development**
USC	**Ulster Special Constabulary**
USCG	**United States Coast Guard**
USCL	**United Society for Christian Literature**
USDA	**United States Department of Agriculture**
USDAW	**Union of Shop, Distributive, and Allied Workers**
USES	**United States Employment Service**
USgal	**US gallon**
USGS	**United States Geological Survey**, part of the Department of the Interior
USI	**United Service Institution**
USIA	**United States Information Agency**
USM	**underwater-to-surface missile**

USM **United States Mail**
USM **unlisted securities market**
USMC **United States Marine Corps**
USN **United States Navy**
USO *(US)* **United Service Organizations**
USP **unique selling proposition**
USP **United States Pharmacopeia**
USPG **United Society for the Propagation of the Gospel**
USR **Universities' Statistical Record**
USS **United States Senate**
USS **United States Ship**
USS **United States Steamer** (*or* **Steamship**)
USSR **Union of Soviet Socialist Republics**
USW **ultrashort wave**
Ut. **Utah**, a US state
UT **unit trust**
UT **Universal Time**, another name for Greenwich Mean Time
UT postcode for **Utah**, a US state
UTA **Unit Trust Association**
UTC ***universel temps coordonné*** (French), Coordinated Universal Time
UTC **University Training Corps**
Utd **United**
ut dict. ***ut dictum*** (Latin), as directed; used in prescriptions
UTI **urinary tract infection**
UU **Ulster Unionist**
UUM **underwater-to-underwater missile**
UUUC **United Ulster Unionist Coalition** (*or* **Council**)
UUUP **United Ulster Unionist Party**
UV *(Physics)* **ultraviolet**
UVF **Ulster Volunteer Force**
Uwist *or* **UWIST** **University of Wales Institute of Science and Technology**
UXB **unexploded bomb**

V

v	symbol for **velocity**
v.	***von*** (German), of; used in names
V	**Liberal Party**, a Danish centre-left political party
V	chemical symbol for **vanadium**
V	**Vatican City**, international vehicle registration
V	**victory**
V	symbol for **volt**, a unit of electric potential or potential difference
V	**volume**
V	Roman numeral for **5**
V.	**Viscount**
V.	**Viscountess**
VA	*(US)* **Veterans' Administration**
VA	**Vice-Admiral**
VA	postcode for **Virginia**, a US state
VAB	**vehicle assembly building**, of NASA
vac.	**vacant**
VAD	**Voluntary Aid Detachment**
VADAS	**voice-activated domestic appliance system**
V-Adm	**Vice-Admiral**
V & A	**Victoria and Albert Museum**, a museum of decorative arts in London
V & V	*(Computing)* **verification and validation**
VAR	**visual aural range**
Varig *or* **VARIG**	**Viação Aérea Rio Grandense** , a Brazilian airline
Vascar *or* **VASCAR**	**visual average speed computer and recorder**
VASP	**Viação Aérea São Paulo** , a Brazilian airline
Vat.	**Vatican**
VAT	**value-added tax**, a tax on goods and services
VAV	**variable air volume**
VAX	*(Computing)* (trademark) **virtual address extension**

vb	**verb**
VC	**Vice-Chairman**
VC	**Vice-Chancellor**
VC	**Vice-Consul**
VC	**Vickers Commercial** ; used on aircraft, e.g. VC10
VC	**Victoria Cross**, a British decoration for conspicuous bravery in wartime
V.C.	**Viet Cong**
VCAS	**Vice-Chief of the Air Staff**
VCDS	**Vice-Chief of the Defence Staff**
VCE	**variable-cycle engine**
VCGS	**Vice-Chief of the General Staff**
VCNS	**Vice-Chief of the Naval Staff**
VCPI	*(Computing)* **virtual control program interface**
VCR	**videocassette recorder**
VCR	**visual control room** (at an airfield)
VD	**venereal disease**
VD	**Volunteer Decoration**
V-Day	**Victory Day**
VDC	**Volunteer Defence Corps**
VDH	**valvular disease of the heart**
VDI	*(Computing)* **virtual device interface**
VDJ	**video disc jockey**
VDQS	***vin délimité de qualité supérieure*** (French), superior quality wine; used on wine labels
VDR	**videodisc recording**
VDRL	**venereal disease research laboratory** (as in VDRL test)
VDT	**visual display terminal**
VDU	**visual display unit**, an electronic output device for displaying the data processed by a computer on a screen
VE	**Victory in Europe**
veep	*(US)* **a vice president**
veg.	**vegetable**
veh.	**vehicle**
Ven.	**Venerable**
VERA	**vision electronic recording apparatus**
verb. sap.	***verbum sapienti satis*** (Latin), a word is enough to the wise
ves. *or* **vesp.**	***vespere*** (Latin), in the evening; used in prescriptions
vet	**veteran**
vet	**veterinary surgeon**

VF *(Medicine)* **ventricular fibrillation**
VF **video frequency**
VF **visual field**
VF **voice frequency**
VFA *(Australia)* **Victorian Football Association**
VFL *(Australia)* **Victorian Football League**
VFD *(US)* **volunteer fire department**
VFT *(Australia)* **very fast train**
VFW *(US)* **Veterans of Foreign Wars**
v.g. *or* **VG** **very good**
VG **Vicar General**
VGA *(Computing)* **video graphics array**
v.g.c. **very good condition**; used in advertisements
VHD **video high density**
VHE **very high energy**
VHF **very high frequency**, referring to radio waves that have very short wavelengths
VHS (trademark) **Video Home System**
VHT **very high temperature**
v.i. *(Grammar)* **verb intransitive**
VIASA **Venezolana Internacional de Aviácon, SA**, Venezuelan International Airways
Vic. **Victoria**, an Australian state
Vice-Adm. **Vice-Admiral**
VID *(Computing)* **virtual image display**
VIP **very important person**
Virg. **Virginia**, a US state
Vis. **Viscount**
Vis. **Viscountess**
VISTA **Volunteers in Service to America**
viz ***videlicet*** Latin), that is to say *or* namely
VJ **video jockey**
VLA **Very Large Array**, the largest and most complex single-site radio telescope in the world, located in New Mexico
VLBW **very low birth weight**
VLF **very low frequency**
VLLW **very low-level waste**
VLR **very long range** (aircraft)
VLSI *(Electronics)* **very large-scale integration**, advanced technology in the microminiaturization of integrated circuits

VM **Victory Medal**
VM **Virgin Mary**
VM *(Computing)* **virtual machine**
V-mail *(Military) (US)* **victory mail**
VM/CMS *(Computing)* (trademark) **virtual machine, conversational monitor system**
VMS *(Computing)* **virtual machine system**
VN **Vietnam** , international vehicle registration
VO **very old** (brandy, whisky, etc.)
VO **Veterinary Officer**
VO (Royal) **Victorian Order**
VOA **Voice of America**
voc. *(Grammar)* **vocative**
vocab. **vocabulary**
voc-ed **vocational education**
vol **volume**
VOP **very oldest procurable** (brandy, port, etc.)
VOR **very-high-frequency omnirange** (*or* **omnidirectional range**)
vox pop ***vox populi*** (Latin), voice of the people
VP **Vice-President**
VP **Vice-Principal**
VQMG **Vice-Quartermaster-General**
VR **velocity ratio**
VR ***Victoria Regina*** (Latin), Queen Victoria
VR *(Computing)* **virtual reality**
VR **Volunteer Reserve**
VRAM *(Computing)* **video random access memory**
VRO **vehicle registration office**
vs. **versus**
VS **Veterinary Surgeon**
VSB *(Telecommunications)* **vestigial side-band**
VSI **vertical speed indicator**
VSO **very superior old** (brandy, port, etc.)
VSO **Voluntary Service Overseas**, a human rights organization that aims to help Third World development by providing opportunities for people with skills to make a practical contribution as volunteers
VSOP **very special** (*or* **superior**) **old pale** (brandy, port, etc.)
VSR **very special reserve** (wine)

VSTOL *or*
V-STOL **vertical/short takeoff and landing**
v.t. **verb transitive**
Vt **Vermont**, a US state
VT **variable time**
VT *(Medicine)* **ventricular tachycardia**
VT postcode for **Vermont**, a US state
VTC **Volunteer Training Corps**
VTO **vertical takeoff** (aircraft)
VTOL **vertical takeoff and landing**
VTR **videotape recorder**
VU **Volksunie** (Flemish), People's Union, a Belgian federalist political party
VU **volume unit**
Vul. *or* **Vulg.** **Vulgate**, of the Bible
v.v. **vice versa**
VVD **Volkspartij voor Vrijheid en Democratie**, People's Party for Freedom and Democracy, a Dutch free-enterprise centrist political party
VVO **very very old** (brandy, port, etc.)
VW **Very Worshipful**
VW **Volkswagen** , a German car manufacturer

WXYZ

w.	*(Cricket)* **wicket**
w.	*(Cricket)* **wide**
W	chemical symbol for **tungsten**
W	symbol for **watt**, a unit of power
W	**west**
W	postcode for **west London**
W.	**Wesleyan**
WA	postcode for **Warrington**
WA	postcode for **Washington**, a US state
WA	**West Africa**
WA	**Western Australia**, an Australian state
WAAAF	**Women's Auxiliary Australian Air Force**
WAAC	**Women's Army Auxiliary Corps**
WAAF	**Women's Auxiliary Air Force**
WAC	*(US)* **Women's Army Corps**
WACC	**World Association for Christian Communications**
WAF	*(US)* **Women in the Air Force**
WAG	**Gambia**, international vehicle registration
WAGBI	**Wildfowl Association of Great Britain and Ireland**
WAGGGS	**World Association of Girl Guides and Girl Scouts**
WAIS	*(Psychology)* **Wechsler Adult Intelligence Scale**
WAIS-R	*(Psychology)* **Wechsler Adult Intelligence Scale – Revised**
WAL	**Sierra Leone**, international vehicle registration
WAN	**Nigeria**, international vehicle registration
WAN	*(Computing)* **wide area network**
W & S	**whisky and soda**
W & T	**wear and tear**
War	**Warwickshire**, an English county
WARC	**World Administrative Radio Conference**
WARC	**World Alliance of Reformed Churches**
Warks	**Warwickshire**, an English county
Wash.	**Washington**, a US state

WASP — **white Anglo-Saxon Protestant**, a common term to describe the white elite in American society
WASP — *(US)* **Women Airforce Service Pilots**
WAT — **weight, altitude, temperature**
WAT — *(Psychology)* **word association test**
WATS — **Wide Area Telecommunications Service**
W. Aus — **Western Australia**, an Australian state
Waves *or* **WAVES** — *(US)* **Women Accepted for Volunteer Emergency Service**
Wb — symbol for **weber**, a unit of magnetic flux
WB — **Warner Brothers**, a film company
WB — **waveband**
WBA — **West Bromwich Albion** (Football Club)
WBA — **World Boxing Association**
WBC — **World Boxing Council**
WBF — **World Bridge Federation**
w.c. — **water closet** (toilet)
WC — postcode for **west central London**
WCC — **World Council of Churches**, an international organization aiming to bring together diverse movements within the Christian church
W. Cdr *or* **W/Cdr** — **Wing Commander**
WCEU — **World Christian Endeavour Union**
WCL — **World Confederation of Labour**
WCT — **World Championship Tennis**
WCTU — *(US, Canada)* **Women's Christian Temperance Union**
WD — **Dominica**, international vehicle registration
WD — postcode for **Watford**
WD — **War Department**
WD — **Works Department**
WDC — **Woman Detective Constable**
WDM — *(Telecommunications)* **wavelength division multiplex**
WDS — **Woman Detective Sergeant**
w/e — **weekend**
WEA — **Workers' Educational Association**, a British institution aiming to provide education for working people
w.e.f. — **with effect from**
WEFT — *(Aeronautics)* **wings, engine, fuselage, tail**

WEN	**Women's Environmental Network**
WES	**Women's Engineering Society**
WES/PNEU	**Worldwide Education Service of Parents' National Educational Union**
WET	**Western European Time**
WEU	**Western European Union, an organization established in 1955 as a consultative forum for military issues among the W European governments**
wf *or* **w.f.**	*(Printing)* **wrong fount**
WF	postcode for Wakefield
WFA	**White Fish Authority**
WFC	**World Food Council**, a UN agency
WFEO	**World Federation of Engineering Organizations**
WFP	**World Food Programme**, a UN agency
WFSW	**World Federation of Scientific Workers**
WFTU	**World Federation of Trade Unions**
WG	**Grenada**, international vehicle registration
WG	**wire gauge**
WG	**Working Group**
WGA	**Writers' Guild of America**
Wg/Cdr	**Wing Commander**
W. Glam	**West Glamorgan**, a Welsh county
W h	**watt hour**
WHA	**World Hockey Association**
w.h.b.	**wash-hand basin**
WHO	**World Health Organization**, an agency of the United Nations established to prevent the spread of diseases and to eradicate them
WI	postcode for **Wisconsin**, a US state
WI	**Women's Institute**, a local organization in country districts of the UK for the development of community welfare and the practice of rural crafts
WIA	**wounded in action**
Wilts	**Wiltshire**, an English county
WIMP	*(Physics)* **weakly interacting massive particle**
WIMP	*(Computing)* **windows, icons, menus, and pointing devices**, describing a type of interface that the operator can manipulate in various ways
Wing Cdr	**Wing Commander**
WIP	**work in progress**

Wipo *or* WIPO	**World Intellectual Property Organization**, a UN agency established to coordinate the international protection of inventions, trademarks, designs, and works of art or literature
Wis.	**Wisconsin**, a US state
WISC	*(Psychology)* **Wechsler Intelligence Scale for Children**
WISC-R	*(Psychology)* **Wechsler Intelligence Scale for Children – Revised**
WITA	**Women's International Tennis Association**
Wizo *or* WIZO	**Women's International Zionist Organization**
WJC	**World Jewish Congress**
WJEC	**Welsh Joint Education Committee**
Wk	**Walk**; used in street names
wkt	*(Cricket)* **wicket**
WL	**St Lucia**, international vehicle registration
WL	**wavelength**
WLA	**Women's Land Army**
WLF	**Women's Liberal Federation**
WLHB	**Women's League of Health and Beauty**
WLM	**Women's Liberation Movement**
WMA	**Working Mothers Association**
WMA	**World Medical Association**
WMC	**Working Men's College**
WMCIU	**Working Men's Club and Institute Union Ltd**
WMO	**World Meteorological Organization**, a UN agency that promotes the international exchange of weather information
WN	postcode for **Wigan**
WNO	**Welsh National Opera**
WNW	**west-northwest**
w/o	**without**
WO	**War Office**
WO	**Warrant Officer**
WOF	*(New Zealand)* **Warrant of Fitness** (for vehicles)
Worcs	**Worcestershire**, an English county
worm *or* WORM	*(Computing)* **write once, read many times**, an optical disc used to store data
WOW	**Women against the Ordination of Women**

WP word processing *or* word processor
WPA Western Provident Association
WPA World Pool-Billiard Association
WPBSA World Professional Billiards and Snooker Association
WPC Woman Police Constable
WPESS within pulse electronic scanning
WPI World Press Institute
wpm *or* **w.p.m.** words per minute
WPMSF World Professional Marathon Swimming Federation
WPPSI *(Psychology)* Wechsler Preschool and Primary Scale of Intelligence
WPT Women's Playhouse Trust
WR Western Region (railway)
WR *(Astronomy)* Wolf-Rayet
WR postcode for Worcester
WRAAC Women's Royal Australian Army Corps
WRAAF Women's Royal Australian Air Force
WRAC Women's Royal Army Corps
WRAF Women's Royal Air Force
WRANS Women's Royal Australian Naval Service
WRC Water Research Centre
WRI Women's Rural Institute
WRNS Women's Royal Naval Service
WRP Workers' Revolutionary Party
WRU Welsh Rugby Union
WRVS Women's Royal Voluntary Service
WS postcode for **Walsall**
WS **Western Samoa**, international vehicle registration
WSCF World Student Christian Federation
WSPU **Women's Social and Political Union**, a British political movement founded in 1903 to organize a militant crusade for women's suffrage
WSTN World Service Television News
WSTV World Service Television
W. Suss **West Sussex**, an English county
WSW west-southwest
wt weight
WTA Women's Tennis Association
WTN Worldwide Television News

WTO **Warsaw Treaty Organization**
WUF **World Underwater Federation**
WUS **World University Service**
WV **St Vincent and the Grenadines**, international vehicle registration
WV postcode for **West Virginia**, a US state
WV postcode for **Wolverhampton**
W. Va. **West Virginia**, a US state
WW **World War**
WWF **World Wide Fund for Nature** (formerly World Wildlife Fund), an international organization established to raise funds for conservation by public appeal
WWMCCS **World Wide Military Command and Control System**
WWSSN **worldwide standard seismograph network**
WWSU **World Water Ski Union**
WWW **World Weather Watch**
Wy. **Wyoming**, a US state
WY postcode for Wyoming, a US state
Wyo. **Wyoming**, a US state
WYSIWYG *(Computing)* **what you see is what you get**, a program that attempts to display on the screen a faithful representation of the final printed output

---

x *(Mathematics)* symbol for **an unknown quantity**
X **Christ**, from Greek letter χ
X Roman numeral for **10**
XC *or* **X-C** **cross-country**
XDR **extended dynamic range** (of cassettes)
Xe chemical symbol for **xenon**
x-height *(Printing)* the typesize of lower-case characters as indicated by the size of a letter **'x'**
XL **extra large**; used on clothing labels
Xmas **Christmas**
XMS *(Computing)* **extended memory specification**
Xn **Christian**
Xnty **Christianity**
XO **executive officer**
XO showing a cognac of superior quality
XP **Christ** *or* **Christianity**, from χ and ρ
XPS **X-ray photoelectron spectroscopy**

xq *or* **XQ** **cross-question**
x ref. **cross reference**
XRF **X-ray fluorescence**
Xt **Christ**
Xtian **Christian**
Xty **Christianity**

---

y. **yard**
y. **year**
Y chemical symbol for **yttrium**
YACC *(Computing)* **yet another compiler-compiler**
YAG *(Electronics)* **yttrium-aluminium garnet**
Yb chemical symbol for **ytterbium**
YC **Young Conservative**
YC&UO **Young Conservative and Unionist Organization**
yd **yard**
YE **Your Excellency**
YES **Youth Employment Service**
YES **Youth Enterprise Scheme**
YFC **Young Farmers' Club**
YHA **Youth Hostels Association**, a registered charity founded to promote knowledge and care of the countryside by providing cheap overnight accommodation
YIG *(Electronics)* **yttrium-iron garnet**
YMCA **Young Men's Christian Association**, an international organization which aims at spiritual, intellectual, and physical self-improvement
YMHA **Young Men's Hebrew Association**
YO postcode for **York**
y.o.b. *or* **YOB** **year of birth**
YOP **Youth Opportunities Programme**, replaced by YTS
YP **young prisoner**
YPTES **Young People's Trust for Endangered Species**
yr **year**
yr **your**
YT **Yukon Territory**, a territory of NW Canada
YTS **Youth Training Scheme**, a one- or two-year course of job-training and work experience for unemployed school leavers aged 16 and 17

YU **Yugoslavia** , international vehicle registration
YV **Venezuela**, international vehicle registration
YVFF **Young Volunteer Force Foundation**
YWCA **Young Women's Christian Association**
YWHA **Young Women's Hebrew Association**

Z symbol for **impedance** (electricity and magnetism)
Z **Zambia** , international vehicle registration
ZA **South Africa** , international vehicle registration
Zanu *or*
ZANU **Zimbabwe African National Union**
Zanu (PF) *or*
ZANU (PF) **Zimbabwe African National Union (Patriotic Front)**
Zapu *or*
ZAPU **Zimbabwe African People's Union**
ZE postcode for **Lerwick**
Zech. *(Bible)* **Zechariah**
Zeep *(Nuclear engineering)* **zero-energy experimental pile**
ZEG **zero economic growth**
Zeph. *(Bible)* **Zephaniah**
ZETA *(Nuclear engineering)* **zero-energy thermonuclear apparatus** (*or* **assembly**)
ZFGBI **Zionist Federation of Great Britain and Ireland**
ZI *(Military)* **zone of interior**
ZIF *(Electronics)* **zero insertion force**
ZIFT **zygote intrafallopian transfer**, a method of artificial insemination
zip, Zip *or*
ZIP **zone improvement program** (US postcodes)
Zn chemical symbol for **zinc**
ZPG **zero population growth**
Zr chemical symbol for **zirconium**
ZRE **Zaire**, international vehicle registration
ZS **Zoological Society**
ZST **zone standard time**
ZW **Zimbabwe**, international vehicle registration